HOW TO WORK A ROOM

A Guide To Successfully Managing The Mingling

SUSAN ROANE

Shapolsky Publishers, Inc.
136 West 22nd Street
New York, New York 10011

A Shapolsky Book

Library of Congress Cataloging-in-Publication Data

RoAne, Susan, 1945-
  How to work a room

  Bibliography: p.
  1. Business etiquette. 2. Business enteraining. 3. Public relations. 4. Interpersonal relations. I. Title. II. Title: How to work a room

HF5387.R6 1988   650.1'3   88-26388
ISBN 0-944007-06-6

Typography by Smith, Inc., N.Y.

This book is dedicated
IN MEMORIAM
to the spirit of three special people.

To Ida Cohen,
my grandmother,
who imparted her wisdom

To Ida B. Harvey,
my "assistant mother,"
who helped raise me

To Sally Livingston,
my "femtor" — female mentor
who was a guiding spirit and role model

Acknowledgements

Writing a book is like giving birth to an elephant—at least it feels that way. The stretch marks are huge, but I was never alone.

Hundreds of people gave me their time, energy, insight and humor in personal interviews—friends and colleagues as well as people I met on planes, around pools, and in line at the supermarket. Special thanks to Judith Briles, who recognized the need for this book and kept reminding me that I was the one to write it, and to my agent, Mel Berger.

And thanks to my friends, who supported me, believed in me, let me hibernate, and then listened even when my brain started turning to mush. I am especially grateful to Lana Teplick, Lois Vieira, Sylvia Cherezian, Joyce "Mumsy" Siegel, Ruthe Hirsch, Marcia Teitelbaum, Gertrude Gurd, Dr. Luann Lindquist, Linda Zatopa, Sherris Goodwin, David Schultz, John Patrick, Rich Portland, Dr. Geraldine Alpert, and to Griggs RoAne, my former husband and present friend, who always believed that I could and should write a book.

Thanks to Lisa Miller and Dr. Irving Siegel for proofreading; to Sue Rugge for research assistance; and to Kerry Davis for proofing, word processing, and giving me my behavior modification rewards: M & M's.

Thanks to Rick Enos, the wonderful taskmaster who encouraged me, kept me on schedule, and called on "deadline days" so I could say, "I did it!"

And to Carol Costello, my editor, fellow Fighting Illini and friend.

Thank you all.

Contents

GET READY!

    "Don't talk to strangers."

    "Wait to be properly introduced."
      (The Scarlett O'Hara Syndrome)

    "Good things come to those who wait."
      (The Prom King/Queen Complex)

    "Better safe than sorry." (Risking Rejection)

    "He/she only wants one thing."
      (The Intercepted Pass)

GO!

Foreword

by Jim Cathcart, C.P.A.E.
Author of Relationship Selling: How to Get and Keep Customers

They say that in this world it's not *what* you know, but *who* you know. No other book I have seen will do more for you than this one in the area of making connections and developing professional contacts.

Exceptional business leaders have one single talent that sets them apart from all others—their ability to develop business friendships. Business friendships can cement an empire, or they can simply make a professional dinner more enjoyable and profitable. Ideally, these friendships are low in tension, high in cooperation, based on mutual trust and the desire of both people to help and support each other.

To develop these kinds of friendships, you need to persuade people that you can make their businesses a little more successful, their days a little easier and, in short, their lives a little happier.

Susan RoAne is not only a master at building business friendships, she is also a master at coaching others to build them. I have watched Susan "work a room" and been amazed at the many ways she finds to generate pleasant conversation, show an interest in others, and develop affinity and contacts with people—even when their points of common interest are not immediately evident.

She has been speaking and conducting her seminar on "Contacts, Connections and Cocktails: How to 'Work' a

Room" for seven years and has worked with tens of thousands of people. Her articles have been published in magazines, newspapers and professional journals.

This book will serve you well. It will show you how to overcome shyness or awkwardness when meeting new people, and how to change strangers into "friends I haven't yet met." It will also give you the tools and confidence to expand these initial contacts into personal and professional friendships that can enrich your business and your life.

I congratulate you on selecting this book. I assure you that it will be pleasant reading, and make meeting new people a source of greater pleasure and satisfaction—for you and for them.

INTRODUCTION

You can tell by the feel of the envelope that it's an invitation to *something*, and you're right. One of your clients is the honorary chairperson for a local charity, and they are throwing a huge fundraiser in two weeks. Not only *should* you go, but many potential clients will be there and it's a chance to meet people and promote your business.

Sounds like fun. But before you even have a chance to think about what you'll wear, a little voice in the back of your head pipes up, "Wait a minute...You'll walk into that enormous ballroom and see thousands of strangers! They'll all know one another, but no one will know you. Who will you talk to? What will you say?" Your teeth start to grind and you gingerly place the invitation in your "Wait and See" file.

You are not alone. This scenario happens daily in offices and homes across the country. It doesn't matter whether the invitation is for a purely social event, a business gathering, or a combination of the two—it's uncomfortable to walk into a room full of people you don't know, especially when you want to make a good impression.

It's also one of the best business and social opportunities

you'll ever run across. The benefits of being able to "work" a room with ease and grace are enormous:

• You feel better about yourself. You approach business or social gatherings with enthusiasm and confidence, knowing that this is an arena where you feel comfortable and productive.

• You make invaluable business contacts, as well as starting friendships that may last your whole life. If you hadn't been able to walk up to people, smile, put out your hand and say "Hi!", those opportunities might have been lost.

• You make other people feel more comfortable, which makes them want to know and possibly do business with you.

I have written this book with one goal in mind: To give you the confidence and the tools to walk into any room and *shine* — whether the event is social or professional, a meeting, party, reunion, PTA committee, or the Inaugural Ball. This book is designed to help you manage these events successfully, mingle with ease, and come away feeling that you have accomplished your own goals and made other people feel good in the process. Everybody wins.

The focus will be on:

• Identifying the "roadblocks" that inhibit us from circulating with ease and comfort, and then eliminating them. For each "roadblock," there is an effective remedy.

• Strengthening confidence and projecting the warmth and sincerity that invite people to open up.

• Practical tips and strategies for starting conversations, establishing communication, and building rapport with "strangers."

"Personal culture will be of greater importance for economic success in the future," says Nathan Keyfitz, Andelot professor of sociology emeritus at Harvard, in *American Demographics* magazine. The most successful people will be those who can communicate best with other people.

In the Eighties and Nineties, effectively communicating what you and your business are all about is not just a "plus," but an essential. Working a room can be your number one marketing strategy. It's some of the best advertising you can get...and it's free.

All of us work rooms. If you've ever been to a wedding or a meeting, you've worked a room—or else come to a deep appreciation of how much easier and more pleasant life would be if you developed this skill. People in my presentations tell me that the most upsetting thing about these events is that everyone *else* seems to be completely comfortable. It just isn't so. Most people don't like entering a room full of strangers for any reason. A party with "strangers" is the Number One Social Fear, according to a study on "Social Anxiety" reported in the *New York Times* (December 18, 1984). Most of us would rather speak in public (Fear Number Two) than attend an event with people we don't know.

In my programs, 90% of the participants admit that they are not comfortable at events where they don't know a good number of people. When I poll only those involved in sales and marketing—presumably one of the most outgoing groups anywhere—this figure only drops to 80%. Less than .0025% say they actually enjoy walking into a room full of strangers. Research shows that 40% of all adults have social anxiety, according to a *New York Times* report on research by Dr.

Bella DePaulo, a psychologist at the University of Virginia ("People Often Can't Judge How They Impress Others." June 30, 1987). At a party with strangers, 75% of adults experience anxiety.

So if you're uncomfortable with the client's invitation to the charity fundraiser, or your first meeting of a professional association, or when a colleague invites you to the Rotary, or when your spouse suggests you come along to the trade show, or when you get the notice of your twentieth high school reunion—you are not alone!

In fact, you're in very good company. It might even be said that if you didn't have some anxiety, *you* would not be normal. Most us want to feel comfortable with other people, even strangers, and will do whatever it takes to minimize the anxiety and move through a crowded room with ease and grace. We want to be comfortable, and to make other people feel comfortable. We want to "manage the mingling" so that we have fun, feel good about ourselves, score some professional points, and feel that even "putting in an appearance" is a good use of our time.

This book is for anyone who has to attend events— parties, meetings, conventions, trade shows, fundraisers, cocktail hours, business meetings, professional dinners, reunions, political gatherings, social evenings, etc. The emphasis will be on business, but the principles hold true for any event and for any age group. This book is for anyone who wants to feel more comfortable working a room.

Working a room is an old political phrase that conjures up images of overweight men in smokey back rooms pressing flesh and cutting deals. That's not what we mean today. When I talk about "working" a room, I mean the ability to circulate comfortably and graciously through a gathering of people—meeting, greeting, and talking with as many of them as you wish; creating communication that is warm and sincere; establishing an honest rapport upon which you can build a friendship; and knowing how to start, how to continue and how to end lively and interesting conversations. There is nothing calculated nor manipulative about working a room. If you don't really care about people, if your warmth, your openness, and your desire to connect with them are not genuine—then no technique in the world will help. People sense the truth; they usually know when they are being manipulated. They also know when you are making a sincere effort to extend yourself to them, and they appreciate it. My guideline is: Go to have fun and enjoy the people. The professional benefits will follow. But *go!*

Working a room is a risk, no doubt about it. Our egos are on the line, and that can be intimidating. It can also be tremendously rewarding, on both a personal and a professional level.

This book is about understanding what keeps us from approaching these events with ease and enthusiasm, and about what we can do to make them comfortable, pleasant, profitable, and even fun. It is about giving ourselves permission to work every room we enter, and to reap the benefits—both personal and professional.

Practice really does make perfect. I encourage you to attend as many events as you can and practice the techniques in this book. Some will work well, and others may not be right for you. But as mom always said, "It couldn't hurt to try!" No one ever died from eating spinach. . .or from going to a charity fundraiser.

You may find that you already know some of the information in this book, or that you already practice some of the techniques. Good! Let the book serve as a reminder, and sharpen your skills as you go along. The more you practice, the better you'll be.

And above all—Enjoy!

GET READY!

Chapter 1

THE ROADBLOCKS: MOTHER'S DIRE WARNINGS

Chapter 1

If working a room is so much fun and so profitable, why do our hearts thump, our palms sweat, and our eyes glaze over when we think about it?

The answer is that many years ago, we learned certain survival techniques at our mothers' knees. Mom gave us these dire warnings with the best of intentions, "for our own good," and everybody agreed that we should heed them. The trouble is, they worked a lot better when we were six years old than they do now that we are twenty, forty, sixty or eighty—and we forgot to turn them off. Now that we're no longer walking home alone from first grade, these dire warnings have changed from safety barriers into roadblocks that prevent us from mingling comfortably and effectively with other people. Mom isn't to blame. She was just doing her job to protect us and we love her for it, but we heard these warnings so often—and perhaps repeated them to our own kids so often—that they began to sound like the truth.

There are five major roadblocks to working a room successfully. Knowing where they come from is the first step to letting them go.

ROADBLOCK #1
—"DON'T TALK TO STRANGERS."

This first roadblock is as American as apple pie. It is often accompanied by a shaking of the index finger. It made sense when our mothers gave it to us, and it makes sense when we give it to our children. We *still* don't want our children to talk to strangers on the way home from school—today more than ever. But it *doesn't* make sense when we're selling a product at a trade show, beginning our first day on a new job, attending a formal ball, or mingling at a professional association meeting where contacts and connections are standing six deep around the room. Yet we often find ourselves standing in the door, paralyzed, with that imaginary finger shaking in our faces and the message "Don't talk to strangers" flashing across our subconscious. So, we don't. Instead, we choose a nice, quiet spot at the hors d'oeuvres table and start nibbling, get very busy with a cup of coffee or a drink, smile nervously around the room at no one in particular—and have an awful time.

We also miss tremendous business, career and social opportunities. Who knows what wonderful person or valuable contact was standing around that room, feeling just as uncomfortable as we were?

Life is too short, and time too precious, to spend an hour or two squandering opportunities and having a bad time in the process.

* * *

ROADBLOCK #2
—"WAIT TO BE PROPERLY INTRODUCED."
(THE SCARLETT O'HARA SYNDROME)

Imagine Scarlett, standing on the steps of Tara in all its antebellum glory, batting her eyelashes as she drawls, "My, but we haven't been properly introduced." Her beauty and charm notwithstanding, Scarlett wouldn't have gotten very far at a professional association meeting.

In Scarlett's day and social sphere, everyone was very much aware of proper introductions and there were people, usually older women, who did little else. They would make *sure* you met that gallant, dark-haired man or that stunning belle.

But tomorrow did, indeed, become "another day" and now you can't count on personal or professional "matchmakers" to be sure you are introduced around at the political meeting or the reception after the lecture. Yet many of us were taught that it "wasn't nice" to talk to someone unless we had been introduced by a mutual acquaintance. It is certainly *easier* to begin a conversation when you've been formally introduced. At the very least, you have in common the person who introduced you. "How do you know Leslie?" elicits more information about the person you've just met, and can lead to other subjects of conversation.

But at most events we can't count on being introduced to anyone, let alone the people we most want to meet. We may be on our own when it comes to circulating, and we may have to walk up to people and introduce *ourselves*. If we don't want to be left standing in the middle of the room, staring at the ceiling or the floor, we have to realize that Scarlett had her world and we have ours. . . and send her packing back to Tara.

ROADBLOCK #3
—"GOOD THINGS COME
TO THOSE WHO WAIT."
(THE PROM KING/QUEEN COMPLEX)

Let's face it. The world may beat a path to the door of Prom Kings and Queens, but not everyone is royal. And once the Prom is over, even the ex-Kings and ex-Queens can't always afford to sit back and hope that people will seek them out.

As we watched the Kings and Queens besieged with dates, mom told us, "Good things come to those who wait." Au contraire. . . gray hair comes to those who wait, and sometimes even varicose veins if the waiting is done standing up!

Waiting for people to find you and introduce themselves is an exercise in futility. Chances are, they won't—because it's just as difficult for them as it is for you. The "waiting game" is a colossal waste of time, no fun at all, and murder on your self-esteem.

It reminds me of myself and legions of other present and former teenagers who sat by the phone and stared at it, waiting for it to ring. I learned the hard way that it did NOT work for the Prom. Why would I expect it to work now?

Even the inventor who actually does build a better mousetrap has to get out there and let people know about it. If he doesn't, he'll sit at home for the rest of his life with no mice, but no fame or fortune either. He might as well have bought a cat.

People who "wait for others to come to them" can often be found in the corner of the room, holding up the walls, envying those who glide around the reception or the cocktail party meeting people.

And let's talk about "pushy." There is pushy, and there is pushy. Obviously, you don't want to throw yourself into a stranger's arms or pin him down on the conference table, wagging your finger in his face and forcing fistfuls of business cards into his pockets. That's one thing. It's quite another to approach someone in a pleasant, friendly way, to smile, introduce yourself, and say something like, "This is my first meeting. Is there always such a good turnout?"

People who fall victim to the Prom King/Queen Complex and sit around waiting for the world to find them have often passively accepted the label "shy." They may or may not actually be shy, but that is how people think of them and that's how they've come to think of themselves.

In one of my early jobs as an elementary school teacher, I found that these labels often became self-fulfilling prophecies. The "Troublemaker" of the class always found a way to maintain that dubious distinction. The "Talker" (today's conversationalist) always managed to get the most red checks next to "Keeps Profitably Busy." (I'm afraid I fell into this category, but to this day I can't imagine anything more compelling about school than social intercourse with my classmates. Multiplication tables? Diagramming sentences? Give me note-passing and furtive whispering in the back row!)

Shyness can be a learned response, according to Dr. Lynne Kelly, a University of Hartford professor who specializes in the study of shyness ("Professor Treats Problem of Shyness," New York Times, February 3, 1985). What we learn, we can unlearn. Working on both communication and conversation skills is one way of unlearning shyness.

"Most people experience 'situational shyness,'" says Kelly's colleague, Dr. Robert Durn. Certain situations make all of us reticent. We may be as shy about an important sales meeting, a product review, or a child's parent-teacher conference as we are about walking into the grand ballroom of a major hotel and having 1,000 people turn their heads in our direction.

But with training, practice, and refining our communication skills, shyness can be reduced or eliminated altogether.

Leaders and successful people have learned to overcome their shyness. They don't wait; they reach out and extend themselves to people. In *The Magic of Thinking Big*, Dr. David Schwartz says, "It's a mark of real leadership to take the lead in getting to know people...It's always a big person who walks up to you and offers his/her hand and says hello."

ROADBLOCK #4
—"BETTER SAFE THAN SORRY."
(RISKING REJECTION)

So you work up your nerve to approach a stranger. You smile, say hello, and introduce yourself. The other person casts you a disinterested glance that screams, "WHO CARES?"

This hurts. No one wants to be rebuffed nor ignored. Our egos are on the line when we extend ourselves to others, because there is always the possibility that they won't be interested in talking with us.

But mother's dire warning that we're "better safe than sorry" puts a real damper on risk, and risk is the name of the game when you are working a room.

I like to think of this risk as a challenge. If you don't have anything on the table, you never win. If you don't take the risk and reach out to people, you never make new friends or contacts. We risk our lives all the time on the freeway. Most of us are strong enough to withstand a temporarily chipped ego.

The truth is, very few people will be openly hostile or rude—if for no other reason than it's bad business.

ROADBLOCK #5
—"HE/SHE ONLY WANTS ONE THING!"
(THE INTERCEPTED PASS)

Mother may have had a point here, but she was probably talking about high school boys in the 1950's. Libidos are inclined to cool, at least somewhat, in the passage from the locker room to the board room.

Still, we run the risk that our warm, open, friendly manner will be misconstrued as an invitation to a liaison. Women are especially vulnerable to this misinterpretation. A touch on the arm that is intended as a simple gesture of understanding can be misconstrued as an indication of sexual interest.

Nevertheless, mother's warning is a bit extreme. We can't walk around with the notion that every member of the opposite sex is ready to pounce on us at the slightest provocation. That would put *us* back into high school in the Fifties...and for me, at least, once was enough. We just don't have the time. We have to go about our lives, be very clear with ourselves about our intent, exercise a bit of caution in this area, and let the chips fall where they may.

RISKING THE ROADBLOCKS

These five roadblocks are part of what stops us from mingling, circulating, and working a room. In the next chapter, we'll discuss specific remedies for each roadblock.

But there is something else that can stop us from moving comfortably around a room, something more subtle than the five particular roadblocks we've just discussed. It has to do with self-perception, self-confidence, and self-esteem. People who register low in these areas can talk themselves out of meeting people and feeling at ease talking to them.

In *Talking To Yourself*, Dr. Pamela Butler deals with the concept of self-talk. These are the things we say to ourselves in our minds, sometimes without even being aware that we are saying them. Self-talk can be either positive or negative. Dr. Butler says that we can change negative self-talk to positive self-talk, and that this transformation can have benefits in all areas of our lives.

Here is some negative self-talk that might come up when you think of working a room:

• I've always had trouble meeting people. It's just the way I am.

• I don't have anything important or interesting to say. I'll just embarrass myself. Better to keep quiet and be cool.

• Why would anyone want to listen to me? All these people have more important things to do.

Take a moment to write down any negative self-talk you may have, and then rewrite those statements into positive ones. The above comments might be rewritten as:

• I'm having fun practicing meeting people, and getting better at it all the time. I'm enjoying mastering a new skill.

• I want to extend myself to other people, and know that the most valuable thing I have to offer is myself. If I'm open and honest, I'll feel good about myself and so will they.

• We're all busy, but everyone enjoys connecting with other people. I'm a valuable, likable person. Extending myself is a gift that others appreciate.

CHANGE IS A RISK

Change of any kind is a risk and feels uncomfortable—even when the change is for the good. It's a little sad to leave the old house, even when we're moving into a much nicer one. We leave behind the old, familiar ways and step onto new ground. No matter how wonderful the change—getting married, expanding your business, moving to an exciting new city, switching careers—there is always a certain amount of discomfort.

For most of us, working a room is a change. But extending ourselves to people is almost always worth the risk. When we try and succeed, it feels like a million dollars. But when we allow negative self-talk to prevail, we can talk ourselves out of taking a risk and become overwhelmed by the roadblocks.

How many times have you seen someone who looked vaguely familiar, but were afraid to go over because he might be not be who you thought he was? I say, so what if I *am* wrong? The worst that can happen is that he says he's not that person and I've make a new acquaintance—possibly a new friend.

In 1981, I attended my first meeting of a local professional association. One of the men there looked like a person I had met the previous June at a career training conference. He was standing alone at the bar. Several questions raced through my mind when I saw him. What if he wasn't the man I had met, but just a look-alike? Would he think I was coming on to him? On the other hand, what if he really *was* the person I'd met and felt slighted that I didn't recognize him? Should I go up and say hello, or wait for him to come to me?

Of all these possibilities, I decided that the worst result would be that he was the person I'd met and thought I was ignoring him. My value system, which includes more than a mild dose of guilt, took over. I approached Farrell Chiles and mentioned the June conference. He was *not* the person I had met, but we had a pleasant conversation.

He had been following the "Careers" series in the *San Francisco Examiner* and remembered several of my columns. That made me feel terrific. I was very glad that I'd overcome my reluctance to approach him. The benefits have been immeasurable. We play significant roles in each other's networks and we are friends. We tell the story of our unique first meeting, and always pay tribute to that great old line, "Don't I know you from someplace?"

Many of my colleagues attend business socials sponsored by local Chambers of Commerce. These are touted as an opportunity to meet other single people in a setting with some propriety. At one mixer a friend spotted a woman who intrigued him. He watched her talking, laughing and enjoying herself. "I really wanted to meet her," he said. "She appeared to be so warm and positive. And she had a great laugh. But all that came to my mind were those self-critical comments that convinced me that she wouldn't like me. So I never even introduced myself. What a loss!"

Another associate had a happier experience. At a holiday party, she decided to "go for it" and ask one of the men she'd met to dance. Deborah (name changed to protect the innocent) had hoped for a more romantic outcome than an exchange of business cards, but that was not the case. She told me she was disappointed, but also congratulated herself for having the courage to risk rejection. She practiced a new behavior...and she survived! Deborah, who thinks of herself as shy, knows that the next time it will be easier.

CORRALLING YOUR COURAGE

No one can give you the courage to introduce yourself to a stranger. But some people are more supportive of that behavior than others. My advice: Stick with those who encourage you to take the initiative.

One way to muster up the courage to take a risk is to ask yourself, "What's the worst that can happen?" Surprisingly enough, your worst fear is usually *not* a matter of life and death. And the odds are that disaster will not occur—and that even if it does, you will survive.

Taking the risk is almost always worth the discomfort. It's a cliche, but "Nothing ventured, nothing gained."

Lisa Miller, a travel planner in Marin County north of San Francisco, said to me at an event, "I realized that the worst possible thing would be that someone wouldn't like me or would laugh at me. And, so what! Of all the other people here, someone will like me! Understanding that gave me confidence to keep trying. And now, it is more fun than it is work."

REMINDERS

"Mother's Dire Warnings" still lurk in our subconscious. These five roadblocks can prevent us from making the most of a party or business event.

- Don't talk to strangers.
- Wait to be properly introduced. (The Scarlett O'Hara Syndrome)
- Good things come to those who wait. (The Prom King/Queen Complex)
- Better safe than sorry. (Risking Rejection.)
- He/she only wants one thing! (The Intercepted Pass.)

Be aware of negative self-talk, and change it into positive self-talk. Extending yourself to people feels risky, but the benefits are well worth the discomfort.

Chapter 2

THE REMEDIES: REMOVING THE ROADBLOCKS

Chapter 2

Now for the good news: For every roadblock, there is a remedy. Those dire warnings can stop us at any time, unless we apply the appropriate remedy.

REMEDY #1:
REDEFINE THE TERM "STRANGER"

Mom says not to talk to strangers? Okay, let's redefine the term. Obviously, we have to exercise some caution in today's society. Not every street corner in town is a suitable place to mix and mingle. And there will always be some people who, for some inexplicable reason, make you feel very uneasy. Go with your gut reaction.

But if you are attending a meeting of professional colleagues, you're not really with strangers. If you go to a PTA meeting, you may not know anyone in the room, but you all have a common interest in quality education for your children. When you go to a new health club, a new church, a new synagogue, a new charitable or political organization, you have a *common interest* with those people.

When you go to a party, you probably know the host or hostess. At a wedding, you have some connection with the bride or groom. At a baseball game, notice how everyone talks to everyone else who is rooting for the same team.

Look for what you have in common with people at an event. This is the planning that helps you feel more comfortable and more prepared. You share interests with anyone who does the same kind of work you do, who is interested in your work, or whose work interests you. People who sell respirators, perform surgery, repair medical equipment, and process insurance have a common collegial bond. They all deal with hospitals. If you volunteer for the local United Way, March of Dimes or public radio station, you have a common interest both with the other volunteers and with people who volunteer for other organizations. People who have children have a common bond—whether they are construction engineers, musicians, used car salesmen, or company presidents.

These common interests can be the basis for conversation. Understanding what we have in common with others takes the edge off our reluctance to approach them as "strangers."

A friend of mine attended a formal fundraiser for his son's school and, in talking with another father whom he knew from Little League, discovered that the other dad did executive search. A happy coincidence, since my friend was planning a career change!

Use common sense when approaching people you don't know, but loosen up the definition of "stranger" so that Mother's Dire Warning doesn't keep you from establishing contacts and communication. Whether you're at a charity awards banquet, a spouse's company dinner dance, or your child's soccer team play-offs, identifying the common ground can help you break the ice.

You will feel more comfortable, and that will be your reward for changing a behavior and breaking through a roadblock.

REMEDY #2:
PRACTICE A SELF-INTRODUCTION

Scarlett O'Hara may have needed a "proper introduction," but we live in a different world. We may never meet another living soul if we wait for a Fairy Godperson or Ed McMahon to appear and introduce us around. We'll just stand in the corner, watching the real "room workers" who seem totally comfortable moving around the room, meeting strangers, conversing and circulating through the crowd.

Every so often, you actually get lucky and attend an event that has a greeting committee. The problem is, not everyone on the committee knows who you are, who you want to meet, or how to introduce people properly—so they may not be able to give you much of an introduction, and they may not give it to the right people. Don't let yourself be limited by their lack of skills, their lack of information, their lack of contacts, or all three.

The truth is that only Johnny gets Ed McMahon to introduce him. The rest of us are on our own. Therefore, we need to have a *planned* and *practiced* self-introduction that is clear, interesting and well-delivered.

What you say about yourself will depend on the nature of the event. At a Chamber of Commerce reception, for example, you should say your name and what you do—with energy. But at a purely social function, your occupation may not be as important as how you know the host or hostess. Your self-introduction should be tailored for the event.

When I attended my neighbor's daughter's wedding, for instance, I didn't use my business introduction as a professional speaker and author—although I was prepared with business cards in my evening bag. Instead, I said warmly (and carefully, because it was a bit of a tongue-twister), "I'm the neighbor. . .of the mother. . .of the bride."

A good self-introduction includes your name and something about yourself that establishes what you have in common with the other people at the event. It doesn't have to be long, only about eight to ten seconds. You don't need the added stress of giving a speech, and you don't want people standing around gaping while you tell them your life story. But your self-introduction should give the essential information, and perhaps something interesting that may engage people in conversation.

- "Hello. I'm Jack Jones. I represent our New York office."
- "Hello. I'm Jennifer Smith, former roommate of the bride."
- "Hello. I'm Karen White. This is my first meeting. Are you a member?"

Your self-introduction may feel a little awkward at first, but after some *planning* and *practice* you'll feel much more at ease with it and have a wonderfully effective remedy for the Scarlett O'Hara Syndrome.

* * *

REMEDY #3:
MOVE FROM "GUEST" BEHAVIOR
TO "HOST" BEHAVIOR

Remember the Prom King/Queen Complex, and Mother's Dire Warning not to be pushy? There is no need to get gray hair waiting for "good things to come to you." Here is a remedy.

Dr. Adele Scheele, author of *Skills For Success*, says that people in a social or networking situation tend to behave either as "hosts" or as "guests."

The "hosts" exhibit gracious manners—meeting people, starting conversations, introducing others and making sure that their needs are met. "Hosts" are concerned with the comfort of others and actively contribute to that comfort.

"Guest" behavior is just the opposite. "Guests" wait for someone to take their coats, offer them a drink, and introduce them around the room. Often, the wait is interminable. If no one performs these services for them, "guests" move to the corners of the room and stand there until someone rescues them. They may be suffering the agonies of shyness, but other people interpret their behavior as "standoffish."

The bottom line is, "hosts" have something to *do* and "guests" do not. Dr. Scheele suggests that the key to success is moving from "guest" behavior to "host" behavior. We all have it in us to be "hosts." After a presentation I gave for the National Speakers' Association in San Francisco, my colleague Winston Hoose asked me, "Susan, how did you learn to work a room?" After a moment's thought, I shrugged my shoulders and told him the truth: "My mother made me!" Most of us were taught the same.

Most of us have entertained in our homes, if only to have people over for beer, pizza, and the game or Academy Awards. Even if we haven't, we've *watched* people entertain—our parents, our friends, or even the maitre d' at a restaurant, who performs many of these same functions. Some people have developed their "hosting" skills more than others, but all of us have some level of what I call "innate host behavior."

What exactly do hosts do? Basically, the host's job is to extend himself or herself to the guests and make them feel comfortable. If you are having company or throwing a party, you plan a guest list and a menu. You clean out the hall closet. When the guests arrive, you welcome them at the door, take their coats and invite them in. You smile and greet them. You offer them food and get them something to drink. You introduce them around, mentioning the things they have in common with other people. You provide conversation starters, perhaps an interesting story or piece of information about the guest. At the end of the evening, you retrieve their coats and thank each guest for coming.

These are things that most of us have done, but we may be out of practice. It may be time to dust off those social skills and start practicing them at public events. The only way to move from "guest" to "host" behavior at events is to DO IT. Try one behavior at a time. You'll start to remember all those things mom drummed into your head, and become more confident with being a "host." I may sound like a Pollyanna, but it feels good to think of someone else's comfort before your own. In the end, it makes *you* more comfortable.

You might try volunteering to be on the greeting committee of your organization. You get to meet everyone who comes in the door; it's your *job* to meet people and make them feel comfortable. You have something specific to do, and it is just the thing you want to do anyway—meet and connect with people. You have an excuse to be as .outgoing as you want to be.

CAUTION: "Acting" as a host will not be successful if it is, indeed, an act. If you really don't care about the people you meet and greet, it will be very evident. "Acting warmly" is a self-contradictory phrase. Either you is...or you isn't.

Moving from "guest" to "host" behavior is the perfect remedy for the Prom King/Queen Complex. It makes the meeting or the evening *your* show. You feel more comfortable extending yourself to others because it is your *job, and others are naturally drawn to you.*

REMEDY #4:
RESPOND TO RUDENESS AS YOU WOULD TO THE FLU—AND FLY THE COOP!

Fear of rejection is sometimes a self-fulfilling prophecy. If we're afraid that people will reject us, they may! Even when it comes at us from out of the blue, it's hard to take. It's no fun to put yourself out, extend a hand and a smile, introduce ourselves, and get a withering stare in return.

The only advice I can offer in response to this kind of rude behavior is to *move on.* Don't try to escalate the battle. The other person is probably ready and willing to "out-rude" you, and there is no point in stooping to his or her level.

Instead, simply walk away. The other person's behavior probably has nothing to do with you; he or she most likely treats a lot of people that way. Respond to this kind of inappropriate behavior as you would a deadly flu bug—and fly the coop!

REMEDY #5:
ANTICIPATE THE "INTERCEPTED PASS" WHILE IT IS STILL ON YOUR END OF THE FIELD

With so many men and women working together today, we have to watch our P's and Q's—or some behaviors that are not intended as sexual will be misinterpreted as such. However, there are several things you can do to prevent your words, gestures, clothing and manner from being perceived as suggestive.

The first is to ask yourself if your behavior really *is* being misinterpreted, or whether you actually do have an interest in this person. If your interest really is romantic, face the truth yourself and proceed in a way that won't jeopardize your professional relationship.

If you *aren't* interested, and you don't want the issue to surface again with someone else:

• Don't dress for misperception. Avoid see-through blouses and other suggestive clothing in the office.

• Stay away from double entendres and off-color comments.

• Be conscious of body language.

• Be clear about your purpose. Stick to business.

• You might even want to "lose your touch" a bit, at least in situations where it is apt to be misinterpreted.

We can't control others' thoughts and actions, but we can be aware of the signals we send—and of whether or not we want to send them.

Continue to be friendly and outgoing...just be aware.

Each of these remedies represents a change in behavior, but you will reap the benefits a hundredfold. We'll talk about some of those benefits in the next chapter.

REMINDERS

The good news about the five roadblocks to working a room is that there is a remedy for each one. With a little practice, a little risk-taking, and some old-fashioned social graces, those Dire Warnings will never again stop you from moving through a room with ease and grace. The added benefits are making good contacts and, most importantly, having a great time.

ROADBLOCK	REMEDY
Don't talk to strangers..........	Redefine the term "stranger."
Wait to be properly introduced (The Scarlett O'Hara Syndrome).	Practice a self-introduction.
Good things come to those who wait. (The Prom King/Queen Complex)....................	Move from "guest" behavior to "host" behavior.
Better safe than sorry. (Risking Rejection).............	Respond to rudeness as you would to the flu, and fly the coop!
He/she only wants one thing! (The Intercepted Pass)..........	Anticipate the "Intercepted Pass" while it is still on your end of the field.

Chapter 3

BENEFITS:
THE BONUSES
OF BEING THERE

Chapter 3

Have you ever been invited to a dinner, reception, or meeting that you couldn't avoid, but that didn't sound very exciting? You write down the event in your calendar, drag yourself there, put in your time, and come home feeling as if you've wasted three hours.

With a little planning, that need never happen again. The event doesn't exist that can't be made productive, or at least fun, if we give it a little thought before we go. It doesn't take much time or effort to turn those "chore" events into "choices" that we approach with enthusiasm.

TURNING CHORES INTO CHOICES

To work a room effectively, we need to know why we are doing it. If there is nothing in it for us or for other people, if there is no goal or purpose—why bother?

If you have decided to work a room, you should know WHY—whether it is a cocktail party, a board meeting, or Parents' Night at your son's high school. The benefits will vary from room to room, depending on the nature of the event, but you should have a clear purpose for attending.

Why have you chosen to spend your time there, instead of doing a report, watching Falcon Crest, practicing your golf swing, helping the kids with their homework, going for a run, or visiting your relatives?

Only one person can answer these questions—YOU.

PLANNING PAYOFFS

Before you attend an event, ask yourself what you would like to accomplish—both on a professional level and on a personal level.

It's important to identify these benefits *before* the event. Remember that "business" events can have personal benefits as well, and that purely "social" events can do wonders for your business. Think about what you want as rewards or compensation. I use the term "compensation" because deriving a benefit is a payment—or payoff—for expending the energy and investing the time.

In my presentations, I give people time to jot down what they feel are the most important personal and professional benefits of working a room. These are the points they make most often:

Professional

1. Perceived as powerful and in control
2. Established communication/connections/rapport
3. Increased resource base/potential clients
4. Gained insight; learned new information
5. Increased business and income
6. Enhanced career opportunities
7. Had fun

Yes, fun is a professional benefit. In fact, the best business people often have the most fun, because they have learned the joys of working a room. What's not to like about getting new business, feeling good about yourself, and enjoying other people?

Personal

1. Comfort
2. Self-confidence
3. New contacts/friends
4. Newly acquired knowledge
5. FUN

THE FUN FACTOR

It's no accident that "FUN" is the bottom line on both lists. Who would want to spend time commuting, parking, circulating, and chatting—just to have a lousy time?

Identifying the potential benefits of a meeting, party, convention or whatever is one of the best ways to motivate, tantalize or prod ourselves into making the most of each event. It builds purpose and confidence, and that leads to even more confidence.

And we're not just there to "get ours." It works both ways. Each of us has something to offer other people as well. We can benefit the other attendees by offering information, advice, an ear, leads, ideas, and whatever seems appropriate or useful to them.

* * *

BELIEVING IN THE BENEFITS

It's important to believe in the benefits, to make them real and vital so that they give us energy and spur us on.

As with everything else about working a room, identifying the benefits gets easier with practice. I often ask people to think about the last event that they attended. I then ask them to identify, with 20/20 hindsight, the benefits to them if they had worked the room effectively. I even give them this short form to fill out. Think of an event you attended recently, and try it yourself.

BENEFITS

EVENT _____

SPONSOR _____

PURPOSE _____

LOCATION _____

ATTENDEES _____

REASON FOR YOUR PARTICIPATION _____

_____

POTENTIAL PROFESSIONAL BENEFITS:

1.
2.
3.
4
5.

* * *

POTENTIAL PERSONAL BENEFITS:

1.
2.
3.
4.
5.

The personal benefits can be at least as important as the professional. Even if you never discuss business, the people you meet while working a room can become lasting friends who enrich your life.

Gary Rosenberg, a Los Angeles events and meeting planner, attended a conference of Meeting Planners International. There he met Ken Solano, an Assistant Dean at Northeastern University, who has become a close friend. "We just clicked and made sure we stayed in touch. If either one of us had not been receptive, our friendship would not have developed," according to Gary.

Networking applies to friendships as well as careers. I met Dr. Johnny Miller, a professor at Kent State, at a professional speakers convention. We stayed in touch and when one of his friends, Charles Amico, moved to San Francisco, he called me and now I have *another* friend.

You may have similar stories of chance meetings and networks of friends. If you stop to think about it, many of them probably came from working a room.

* * *

ACCUMULATING CONTACTS:
THE MILLIONAIRE'S ROLODEX

Being able to work a room effectively has one benefit that is extraordinary and unique: You can build an enormous Rolodex. You're on your way to having something in common with millionaires. Georgia State professor Thomas Stanley studied 2,000 millionaires for his forthcoming book, *Marketing to the Affluent*. He found that a huge Rolodex was one of the important traits they had in common.

He also says that these people have an "uncanny ability to distinguish quality contacts." They don't just collect business cards; they can identify the people who are able and willing to help them, the people with whom they can share support, information, and possibly business. A huge Rolodex is useless unless, like the millionaires Stanley studied, we see it as a resource pool of people, ideas and advice.

Working a room is one sure way to expand your contacts. According to Stanley, these millionaires show the same guts and courage in talking to people at events as they do in conducting their businesses.

IT WORKS BOTH WAYS

Remember: We sometimes forget that each of us has something to offer. We can benefit the other attendees by offering information, advice, an ear, leads, ideas, etc.

* * *

REMINDERS

We can learn to approach any event with purpose and enthusiasm if we take the time to look at potential benefits before we go. These benefits can be personal or professional, or both. Having fun and meeting new friends can be just as valuable as striking deals. Working a room effectively has the added and unique benefit that you enlarge your base of contacts and friends, and begin to develop "The Millionaire's Rolodex."

Chapter 4

THE DYNAMIC DUO: CHARM & CHUTZPAH

Chapter 4

Working a room successfully depends on seeing the roadblocks, responding with the appropriate remedies, and identifying the potential benefits. But in the end, what gets us through the night is the dynamic duo of CHARM and CHUTZPAH.

I can hear it now: Charm and Chutzpah in the same breath?

They're a contradiction in terms...and behaviors.

Not true!

CHUTZPAH—THE COURAGE TO CONVERSE

The old, negative connotations of "chutzpah" are gall, nerve, a brassiness that is intrusive and offensive. To me, chutzpah is not aggression, rudeness, disrespect or bulldozing. It is simply the courage to take risks.

Chutzpah allows us to make that first, icebreaking comment, that opens the doors to conversation. It gives us the courage to walk into the party, fundraiser, aerobics class or meeting, take a deep breath, and introduce ourselves to someone.

Can it help you work a room? What else *is* working a room?

Would you wish it on your children? You bet! They will be ahead of the game when *they* start working rooms (and they *will*).

CHUTZPAH IS THE CORNERSTONE OF CONFIDENCE

In the 1980's, chutzpah has been elevated to the status of a management tool. In "Getting Chutzpah" (*Savvy*, November, 1982), psychologist Elliot Jaffa identified chutzpah as an "overlooked personal quality that makes a successful manager."

Jaffee says that chutzpah allows us to risk rejection, ask for what we want, and express ourselves. It gives us the strength to pick ourselves up, dust ourselves off and start all over again.

CHARM—YOU AND THE QUEEN MUM

Here is what Webster has to say about charm:
Verb: To captivate, delight, attract, please
Noun: A power to gain affection
These definitions make most people shout, "Where do I sign up?"

In "charm" school, I was taught how to dress, walk, apply makeup, smile, behave, and be well-mannered. These things are important, but charm includes something more, an elusive quality which draws us to people and makes us believe they care about us. It's easier to define charm in terms of who has it and who does not.

President Nixon doesn't have it; President Reagan does. Mike Ditka doesn't have it; Sugar Ray Leonard does. Bette Davis doesn't have it; Helen Hayes does.

Charm is a combination of warmth, good nature, positive attitude, a good sense of humor, charisma, spirit, energy, and an interest in others. My friend and associate Sherris Goodwin has it. When she owned the Fay Mansion Inn, every guest felt welcomed. People want to be around her. Charm is the ability to convey a type of caring that comes from the heart and soul.

An advice columnist once defined "class" as the "ability to make people of all walks of life feel comfortable." To me, that definition also applies to charm. The person who personifies charm for me is the Queen Mother (Mum) of England, Queen Elizabeth II's mother. Robert Lacy, author of *Queen Mother*, described her on the Today Show as having the "gift of making you feel she's been *waiting all week* to meet you." That truly is a gift—the art of conveying interest, concern and caring for another person.

When we work a room, a party, a convention or a jogging track, we must be keenly aware of other people's feelings. Ignoring someone because the title on their nametag doesn't impress us is a cardinal sin.

ONE AND ONE IS THREE

When chutzpah and charm come together, it's synergistic. The whole is greater than the sum of its parts. You don't just have chutzpah *and* charm; you have MAGIC!

You care about people, and you have the courage to walk up to them and let them know it. That's a powerful combination, and one that enriches everyone concerned.

The dynamic duo of chutzpah and charm isn't a "to do" or a technique. It is something we all have, and that we've developed to a greater or lesser extent. Now is the time to let it out and spread it around.

There is no more effective way to work a room.

REMINDER

Chutzpah and charm are the dynamic duo at the heart of working a room successfully. We all have these qualities. Practice makes them stronger. They let us work a room with style and grace—and ultimately, are what attract people to us.

Chapter 5

The people who are the most successful at working a room are those who genuinely like, respect and trust people. When we don't really care about people, they sense the insincerity and rarely take kindly to it.

BEING "SLIMED"

At a recent benefit, a man who is very involved in his community approached me and told me that he "really knew how to work a room and had a great deal of experience at it." He appeared to be knowledgeable, charming and smooth—on the surface. But as we spoke, his eyes moved around the room to see who else was there, and I sensed he wasn't about to waste time with people he didn't consider important.

Everything he did seemed calculated. He heard my words and responded, but he didn't really listen. When *he* spoke—mostly about himself, his past, his ideas, his successes, his goals—he locked me in with eyes that felt like lasers. Like Bill Murray in *Ghostbusters*, "I felt like I'd been slimed!" Mr. Sleaze was a user and a loser.

Chronicle Features

870 MARKET ST . SAN FRANCISCO . CA, 94102

Week of April 11, 1988

Keeping Up

© Chronicle Features, 1988

Mr. Lapham is going to be our sleaze factor.

MR. OR MS. SLEAZE'S DISGUISES

We've all met The Sleazes at parties, meetings and conferences. They may wear $1,000 Brioni or Chanel suits instead of the proverbial "sharkskin." They may look perfectly conservative and stylish. They may even appear to be the Prince or Princess of our personal or professional dreams. And they may say all the right things.

But you just *know* they don't really care about you or your career, and they almost never follow through with what they promise. Their behavior does not support their words. University educator Ernie Baumgarten told a seminar group, "Behavior that doesn't support words actually subverts them." If what we *do* doesn't support what we *say*, we're worse off than if we hadn't said anything at all.

The Sleazes of the world come in many forms. They are male and female; young, old, and middle-aged; wealthy and struggling. They can be anyone. The common denominator: They have no respect for anyone who can't "do something for them." They are just trying to make their CONTACT QUOTA; and, it shows.

LEARNING FROM SLEAZE

Is there a lesson in Mr. or Ms. Sleaze's behavior? You bet. The technical skills of working a room are *not* enough; the warmth and desire to help must be genuine and sincere.

I hate to sound like Grandma, but when in doubt, apply The Golden Rule. Treat other people as you would want to be treated. It's old-fashioned, but it's easy, true, and almost failsafe.

I say "almost" failsafe because there are some people—
only a few, fortunately—who don't care how we treat them,
because they don't care about *us*. They treat everyone with
a chilling combination of disregard and disdain, and don't
expect anything different from others. They are the Roadblock #4 people who tempt us not to Risk Rejection. All you
can do is apply Remedy #4 and move on.

NO JOKING MATTER—
HUMOR THAT HURTS

The jokester who works a room with inappropriate
humor has the same effect as insect repellent.

An associate whom I will call Linda attended a business
reception where she encountered a local attorney who was
active on the organization's education committee. This Mr.
Sleaze prototype made quite an impression...for his
offensive sense of humor. "Gary came up to me when I was
talking to another woman business owner," Linda told me.
"He said hello and asked me how I was. I hadn't been to our
committee meeting that month due to a severe case of the
flu. So when he asked how I was, I said that I was feeling
much better. Laughing at his own 'wit,' he replied, 'Aren't you
glad *that* time of the month is over? Ha, Ha!' The sad thing
is that he actually thought he was funny. My friend and I
were both so offended! We simultaneously rolled our eyes
and walked away from 'Mr. Bug Spray.' His idea of humor was
insulting. You can be sure I would never refer any business
to him. And if anyone asked me about him, I would be
deafeningly silent."

FATAL FLAWS

There is good news and bad news for Mr. and Ms. Sleaze. The good news is that, if being remembered is the goal, they achieve it. People do remember.

The bad news is that they are remembered for all the wrong reasons. The Sleazes leave a negative impression, and that rarely enhances one's social life or business network.

In addition to being remembered as an insincere user and an unfeeling manipulator, Mr. or Ms. Sleaze often brings to the meeting or party a whole bag of unpleasant social "tricks." These fatal flaws include:

- Disparaging or "put-down" humor
- One drink too many
- Monopolizing someone's time
- Wearing a T-shirt or jeans at a suit-and-tie event
- Wearing a low cut, revealing, or unfashionably tight dress at a business function
- Moving around the room with a cigarette or cigar in hand
- Overloading his/her plate at a buffet and returning too many times
- Eating, drinking and talking simultaneously
- Sizing people up by the title on their nametag (and moving away *conspicuously* if they aren't "important" enough or perceived as a "Decision-Maker)
- Patronizing any individual or group— especially women, the elderly, minorities, or the physically challenged

- Loudness
- The hard sell
- Not following through on offers or promises
- Complaining—about the room, the food, the other attendees, etc.

HOW TO HANDLE A SLEAZE

Extricate yourself...quickly. There is no reason for you to put up with this kind of behavior, nor to waste your time being gracious to someone who doesn't even know or care that you are being gracious to them. Try to be polite, but remember that a Sleaze isn't terribly sensitive to the difference between polite and impolite. The most important thing is to get away.

REMINDERS

Mr. or Ms. Sleaze can show up anywhere, and can come in a variety of disguises. You will recognize them by their uncanny ability to make others uncomfortable, by their concentration on themselves rather than on other people, by their offensive humor and/or behavior, and mostly by their lack of genuine caring or follow-through.

The best way to handle a Sleaze is to extricate yourself from the situation as quickly as possible, and move on to more pleasant company.

GET SET!

Chapter 6

PREPARATION: PLANNING YOUR PRESENCE

Chapter 6

You're set to go! You've identified the roadblocks, applied the remedies, seen the specific benefits of working the room, polished up your chutzpah and your charm, and learned to avoid either resembling or spending time with Mr. or Ms. Sleaze.

What's next? Before you rush out into the night—or the afternoon, or the morning—take some time to PREPARE yourself.

The old Army saw about the five P's also holds true for business and social events: PRIOR PLANNING PREVENTS POOR PERFORMANCE.

Barbara Walters stresses the importance of preparation in How To Say Practically Anything To Practically Anybody. Unlike some interviewers, she doesn't make do with the information provided by the producer or research department. She does her own research, and it is extensive enough that she is almost never taken by surprise. She always prepares more questions than she will have time to ask—whether she is interviewing Anwar Sadat, Jimmy Carter or Elizabeth Taylor. She says that doing your homework is as essential for a successful party as it is for interviewing heads of state.

Whether the event is a cocktail party, a political fundraiser, a dinner meeting, a conference or a reunion, *be prepared.*

SEVEN STEPS FOR PLANNING YOUR PRESENCE

You have to do your homework. You have to know what the event is, who is sponsoring it, and who will attend. Before you leave for any event, be sure to check your wallet, your grooming, and these seven steps:

STEP #1— ADOPT A POSITIVE ATTITUDE

Your attitude can make the difference between an event that is pleasant and successful—and one that ranks with the sinking of the Titanic. Unless you've been blessed (or cursed) with a poker face, it is extremely difficult to mask a negative attitude.

If you go to an event thinking, "Well, I have to be here but I just know I'm going to have a bad time," or "I should really be home working on that budget," or "I'm exhausted; I need a Mental Health Day instead of this reception"—people will know it.

If for some reason you really can't or don't want to go to an event, then DON'T. You owe it to yourself to satisfy your own needs first, and the fact that you don't want to be there will show on your face. Even if you plaster on a smile, it will show in your eyes. It's better not to attend at all than to leave a negative impression.

Why waste a new shirt, or a freshly cleaned silk dress, or the *time* it takes to attend an event if you don't plan to enjoy yourself?

The only people who consistently go to events intending to have a bad time are those who suffer from what I call the "Lemon Sucker Syndrome."

You can identify these people by the look on their faces—excruciating pain, for no apparent reason. Lemon Suckers are miserable, and they *love* their misery! If you try to cheer them up, they'll hate you for it. You may have a Lemon Sucker in your office or in your family. Even those of us who are not Lemon Suckers can occasionally look that way unless we prepare a positive attitude before the event. And most people have enough experience with the Lemon Sucker Syndrome that they will give us a wide berth if they see that uninviting look. We check our makeup and straighten our ties before going out. A positive attitude is even more important, and deserves at least as much attention. I'm not saying you have to bubble like a high school cheerleader in order to appear upbeat, pleasant and positive. A little bit of enthusiasm and a smile go a long way.

The best way I know to generate enthusiasm, if it is not already there, involves Step #2.

STEP #2—
FOCUS ON THE BENEFITS OF THE EVENT

In Chapter Three, we discussed the importance of knowing WHY you are attending a meeting, party, dinner or reception. Your purpose will vary from event to event, but you must know what you stand to gain from leaving your home or office and working the room. Your goals will keep you on track.

Is your purpose in attending this event to be visible among your peers? To show the boss that you support her favorite community project? To be a role model for your employees and demonstrate the importance of participating in the trade association?

I attend events sponsored by my local Chamber of Commerce and by the Convention & Visitors Bureau in order to stay visible and to reconnect with my business buddies. My purpose is not to book speaking engagements, but to touch base with my business and social networks and to have fun.

It is perfectly acceptable to attend an event because you have to—as long as you've prepared a positive attitude. Even among the "Me Generation," the purpose for going to an event may be that "duty calls." Just as on Mother's Day and Thanksgiving, there are certain events where our presence is expected, and the goal may be to fulfill this obligation.

That doesn't mean you have to have a bad time. Even if you "have to" attend a certain cocktail party, you can also focus on the benefits of meeting new people, exchanging conversation and bringing back some business cards to expand your network.

Before the event, take some time to fill out an index card like this one. If you find that your list of benefits continues on the back of the card, so much the better!

You might even slip the card into your purse or wallet, and sneak a look at it before you enter the room. It will remind you of your focus, and of how you are being compensated for your time—in non-monetary and perhaps even monetary terms.

EVENT:	LOCATION:
SPONSOR:	
ATTENDEES:	

Reasons for Participating:	
Professional Benefits:	Personal Benefits:

A WORD OF CAUTION: Be *guided* by your goals, not *blinded* by them. We all know people who are on their way to their goals, and God help anyone who gets in their way! These people don't usually attract others to them, or work a room with much success. Focusing on the benefits of an event helps generate enthusiasm and keep us on track, but genuine warmth and interest in other people are what make us succeed.

STEP #3—
PLAN YOUR SELF-INTRODUCTION

The best self-introductions are energetic and pithy—
no more than ten seconds long. They include your name
(obviously) and a tag line that tells other people who you are
and gives them a way to remember you.

You will probably want to use different self-introductions
for different events.

John Doe, the new Director of Development for
Memorial Hospital, might use these variations:

• At his first meeting of the Development Directors'
Association, where everyone in attendance is a Director of
Development, he might say, "I'm John Doe from Memorial."

• At a cocktail party to introduce administrators to new
Board members, he would say, "I'm John Doe, Development."

• At his daughter's wedding, "I'm John Doe, Mary's
father."

These introductions are pretty basic. It helps to include
a little humor. At the introductory meeting of a non-smoking
seminar, John might say something like, "I'm John Doe, and
I consider myself this program's greatest challenge."

Your self-introduction has two purposes: 1) to tell people
who you are, and 2) to give them a pleasant experience of
you. Speak clearly and *look people in the eye.* Your introduction can be "just the facts," or it can be laced with humor

and perhaps even some information that will stimulate conversation. But in the final analysis, what people will remember is the interest, warmth and enthusiasm they feel from you.

STEP #4—CHECK YOUR BUSINESS CARDS

Before there were business cards, there were calling cards, and their function was similar. Handing out business cards tells people your name, company and position, and gives them a way to contact you in the future.

Some people take business cards for granted. They grab a fistful before leaving their home or office, give some out if others happen to ask them for one, and collect other people's cards at the bottom of their purse or in the deep recesses of their wallet. Some time later (a week to three years) and for whatever reason (usually a new purse or wallet), these potentially valuable resources surface—dog-eared and well on their way to biodegrading from a visit to the cleaners.

This is not the purpose of business cards. The purpose of business cards is to give people a tangible, physical way to remember you and something they can slip directly into their Rolodexes. This is also how you should use *other* people's cards.

* * *

GUIDELINES FOR BUSINESS CARDS

1. *Make sure that your name, your company name, and your phone number are readable.* Select a type face that is big

enough and clear enough so that even Baby Boomers who are now turning forty don't need a magnifying glass or four-foot arms to read your card. (It's not kind to make us over-forty-year-olds feel that our "eyes are going.")

2. *Devise a system for carrying your own cards and for collecting cards from others.* I use a large cigarette case, with a baseball card to divide my cards from those I've collected. If you are comfortable with using a computer to organize the cards when you get back to your home or office, by all means do so. If you are part of the Not Yet Computer Literate Set, as I am, clip the cards together by event and date. That way you can reach into your business card file box and—once you remember the event—you're home free. Filing a card is helpful only if you can retrieve it by remembering the person's name and why you wanted to contact that particular person. Tip #3 will help you remember.

3. *Write a mnemonic device on the other person's card—as soon as possible—to help you remember who they are.* Dennis Berkowitz, owner of Max's Opera Cafe in San Francisco, hosted a Chamber of Commerce business social. He served the most gorgeous smoked fish . . . and I told him so! He wrote "SMOKED FISH" on my card and, three years later, still calls me The Smoked Fish Lady. While this is not my favorite way to be remembered, he does let me know whenever he is having a special shipment of smoked fish flown in from New York.

4. *Bring enough cards.* I learned from my "femtor," the late Sally Livingston, that no one wanted to take home a used napkin—even if it had my name and number on it. Napkins don't fit into anyone's Rolodex. The excuse that "I just gave out my last card" is questionable and smacks of poor planning. No one is impressed by how many people we met moving down the buffet from the brie to the meatballs.

5. *Never leave home without them!* As mom says, "You never know who you'll run into." I keep business cards in the pocket of my running suit!

6. *Do NOT pass out brochures.* Brochures are expensive. They are meant for people who are genuinely interested in doing business with you. They are also bulky. People at a reception have no place to put them, and nobody wants to leave looking like they should have brought a shopping cart. Brochures are also a great way to follow up, so don't waste that opportunity by giving them away at the first meeting.

7. *If you want to give your card to someone but they have not asked for it, ask for theirs first.* Most people will respond in kind, especially if you hold your own card conspicuously, as if you are ready to trade.

8. *Avoid "sticky" situations.* Don't reach for the buffet with one hand and your card with the other. No one wants to take home a card caked with sweet and sour sauce.

9. *Pass out your cards discriminately.* Not everyone should have your business card. Keep your own safety and sanity in mind. *The exchange of cards should follow a conversation in which rapport has been established.* Don't hand them out on the bus, and don't give them to people in whom you can barely detect a pulse. Ask yourself if you actually want this person to call you.

STEP #5—
PREPARE YOUR SMALL TALK

Some people cringe at this idea. They don't like the notion of preparing conversation, and they say that small talk is trivial. I say, "How do you start a conversation with a stranger? With the famine in Ethiopia?" Hardly.

Whether the event is social or professional, there may be no special host to ease you into the room and help begin conversations. You may be on your own.

Small talk gets you through the challenge of "What shall I say next!?" It allows you to learn about other people. If you think about what has been said and respond, you're communicating. Small talk is absolutely essential; it is a way of finding mutual areas of interest.

SILENCE IS NOT GOLDEN

In *The Art of Conversation*, James Morris points out that although we "realize that it is bad manners to monopolize a conversation, it's equally bad manners not to talk enough." Michael Korda, author of *Success, Power & Queenie*, is the nephew of movie magnate Sir Alexander Korda. Korda says that one of the things his uncle had going for him was that he never let things get *too serious*. In an article on small talk in *Signature* (September, 1986) Korda says, "A bore is someone who has no small talk...Silence is not golden—it is the kiss of death."

In this same article, Korda discusses the difference between small talk and large talk: "Large talk is for business negotiations, medical matters, things that involve money, health, life, the law...Small talk should intrigue, delight, amuse, fill up time pleasantly. Given that, anything will do, from dogs to delicatessen. The aim of small talk is to make people comfortable—to put them at their ease—not to teach, preach or impress. It's a game, like tennis, in which the object is to keep the ball in the air for as long as possible."

You will walk into a room with more confidence if you have at least three pieces of small talk prepared—light conversations that you can have with anyone you meet. An exchange of pleasantries makes everyone feel more comfortable before you begin to think on your feet.

You might include a statement, a question, or a pleasant self-revelation. The topics might include a local sports team, the organization for which you are meeting, or even the weather! You will have *something* in common with these people, simply because you are attending the same event. It's best to avoid controversial subjects like politics and religion, but you will probably find several areas of common interest if you look.

Being a good conversationalist includes being a good listener. Get people to talk about themselves and listen with your ears and with your *face*. Conversations are best when both people try to find common areas and are genuinely interested in one another.

Serious discussions have their place, and you may enjoy deep, probing talk with your friends, but small talk can be a good way to break the ice and *begin* friendships.

More later in Chapter 8 about starting, continuing, and ending conversations.

STEP #6—
REMEMBER EYE CONTACT AND A SMILE

"It's good to meet you" is only believable if your warm, sincere smile matches your words. This line doesn't play very well through a frown, or even through a look of indifference.

Eye contact is critical in building rapport. A colleague and his wife recently attended a birthday party for one of her associates. My friend told me later that the "Birthday Boy," a middle manager for a bank, never looked him in the eye as he shook his hand. He all but said, 'I'm looking for someone more important to talk to.' My colleague said, "I was ticked off. How did he know I wasn't more important—or would be someday?"

A roving eye gives the impression of an insincere, hand-pumping Mr. Sleaze.

But a word of caution...Eye contact does not mean *glaring* or staring, which can be rude. Glaring rarely builds rapport or enhances communication. David Givens suggests in *Success* magazine (April, 1985) that we alternate between looking at the person and looking away in order to display just enough interest, and also just enough vulnerability to be approached. Cultural standards vary, but in the United

States a comfortable range is looking for seven seconds, and then looking away for the same time span. Beyond that, the "looking" may become a glare or the "looking away" may suggest that we're scanning the room for better opportunities.

We learn a lot about other people from their eyes, and show them a lot about ourselves with ours.

STEP #7—
PRACTICE YOUR HANDSHAKE

A handshake is the business greeting in America. Jellyfish need not apply here. A firm clasp is the handshake of preference for *greeting* people, *agreeing* to a deal, and *departing* as friends.

These are some handshakes to *avoid:*

1. *The Jellyfish.* A limp hand moves your way. You grasp it and it turns to mush. Do you want to do business with this person? People with jellyfish handshakes create the impression that they are spineless—an unsavory perception, to be sure.

2. *The Knuckle Breaker.* Your hand disappears into a vice and comes back the worse for wear. So the person could play linebacker for the Chicago Bears...do you care? This kind of power play is best left to members of the Mafia. In recent years, some women have adopted The Knuckle Breaker in an effort not to be perceived as pushovers. Women do need to have firm handshakes, but it is doubly disconcerting to extend your hand to a 5'1, 103 pound woman in a silk dress and have it come back feeling like hamburger.

3. *The Finger Squeeze*. This person doesn't clasp your hand; he or she grabs your *fingers only*. When done with a light touch, this gesture appears prissy and/or suggests that the person isn't sure he wants to touch your *whole* hand. With a heavy touch, The Finger Squeeze can become The Ring Squeeze. Marks from your ring are clearly etched in at least two other fingers, and you wonder if you should leave the reception and get an x-ray.

4. *The Covered Handshake*. In this handshake, one of the parties puts his or her left hand over the hands clasped in the handshake. This may be perceived as a show of warmth by those of us who are "touchers." But others may see it as a power play or feel that they are being patronized.

There may be times when a covered handshake is perfectly appropriate. Be sensitive to other people's responses, and let your intuition be your guide.

We don't want to become overly analytical. Several years ago, a Ford Fellow and I were doing some consulting on the same project. He pointed out that I touched people as I spoke, and very seriously told me that this was "a schematic organizational powerplay."

"How interesting," I replied. "And all this time I thought it was because I am a fourth-generation toucher!"

Since it's not always easy to read people or to assess their reaction to a covered handshake, play it safe and stick with the traditional firm clasp, with no left hand playing around the edges.

Men, Women and Handshakes. Men have been trained from childhood to shake hands. Women must master the art as well. It's up to the woman to *extend her hand first* whether she is meeting a man or another woman. Men are taught to wait and see if the woman initiates a handshake. A woman never conveys a mixed message by extending her hand to a man—unless, of course, she is wearing a see-through blouse!

The Business Kiss. To Miss Manners' horror, kissing has also become a business greeting in certain industries. "Bussing for business" is common in the entertainment, hospitality, and human resource fields. People involved in banking, manufacturing, accounting, and the law are less likely to be seen blowing one another little "air kisses."

Marilyn Moats Kennedy covers this subject thoroughly in *Kennedy's Career Strategist* (February, 1986). She says that people living in large cities are more likely to use the business kiss than those in small towns, and offers the following guidelines:

1. Women should not leave lipstick on the kissee. Touch cheeks and kiss the air.

2. In the USA, the business kiss is never delivered on the lips.

3. The person who speaks first usually kisses first. It is acceptable for a man to initiate a kiss because, in theory, business kissing is non-sexual.

4. Business kisses are usually exchanged outside the office—at a convention, for instance. In the office, it is usually not done.

So, never in the office, and never on the mouth. Other than that, let your intuition be your guide. If you think the other person might be uncomfortable, or that you might be subjecting yourself to office gossip, make do with a handshake.

The Kareem Abdul Jabbar Solution. If *you* are uncomfortable and want to avoid the kiss as a business greeting, simply stand as far away from the other person as the length of your arm. Extend your hand, *smile*, and lock your elbow. If Kareem did this, he would keep people about five feet away from him. It's a good way to give yourself some "breathing space" and still make others feel welcome.

REMINDERS

Taking the time to "be prepared" can be the best investment you make. You approach the event with more confidence and certainty, knowing that you are ready for the basics and can move on to the creative. Remember the seven steps for planning your presence.
  1. Adopt a positive attitude
  2. Focus on the benefits of the event
  3. Plan your self-introduction
  4. Check your business cards
  5. Prepare your small talk
  6. Remember eye contact and a smile
  7. Practice your handshake

Chapter 7

SEVEN STRATEGIES: FROM JUMP START TO SMOOTH STOP

Chapter 7

You've done your preparation, but what if your internal engine starts to stall at the thought of actually walking in the door?

These seven strategies will give you a quick jump start and bring you through the event to a smooth stop.

STRATEGY #1—
THE ENTRANCE: GRAND OR OTHERWISE

What time should you arrive? Arrival time is usually based on the starting time of the event—not on making a conspicuous entrance. There is no such thing as being "fashionably late" to a meeting.

When you arrive at the event, take a deep breath, stand tall, and walk *into* the room. Hanging out in the doorway creates a fire hazard, a traffic problem, and the impression that you're timid about coming in.

There may or may not be an official greeter. Anticipate that there will *not* be one, and enjoy the pleasant surprise if there is. Speaker and author Judith Briles recommends volunteering to be on the greeting committee yourself. "That way, you get to meet everyone because it's your job." If you are shy, this gives you something to say to people right away.

Give the room a quick once-over. Where is the bar? Where is the food? Where are people congregating? Where can you position yourself to meet the most people?

A professional speaker who addresses audiences of thousands once told me he had great difficulty attending cocktail parties and talking to people one-to-one. His solution is to position himself between the entry and the buffet table so that everyone has to walk by him to get to the food. He is always surrounded by people.

Once you are in the room, look around for people you know. If you see someone who looks vaguely familiar, go up and introduce yourself. Find out if that person is who you thought he or she was. There is no point in wondering, "What would happen if. . ." One of two things will happen: 1) You'll be right and renew the acquaintance, or 2) You'll meet a new person, chat for a while and move on.

STRATEGY #2—
THE BUDDY SYSTEM

If the thought of entering a room gives you the shakes, try the Buddy System. Make a deal with a friend who must also attend these events, and go together. But don't limit your arrangement to "having someone with whom to walk in the door." The Buddy System can be a great way to work a room—if you do some prior planning and strategizing.

* * *

BUDDY STRATEGIES

1. One of the main advantages of going to an event with a buddy is that you can introduce one another around. You may know people your buddy doesn't know, and vice versa. Even if neither of you know *anyone*, you'll both meet people in the course of the event and can introduce each other to your *new* friends. Brush up on your introduction skills so that you present your buddy as a pleasant, interesting person who has something in common with the other attendees. This means listening to people to find out what their interests are. Give people enough information about your buddy to begin a conversation, and use a positive tone of voice.

2. Make sure your buddy does the same! Your buddy's introduction of you should be as enthusiastic and informative as yours is of him or her. I failed to do this once. A colleague and I agreed to promote each other with our introductions. My introduction of her had her one wave short of walking on water, but her "enthusiastic" introduction of me sounded like a preview of my eulogy. It was deadly. Don Hansen, a San Francisco business consultant, says that some people are "legitimizers," simply by virtue of who they are and how they introduce other people. They are individuals with a certain amount of status, and they know how to present other people to best advantage.

3. You and your buddy will want to split up as soon as possible. If you behave like Siamese twins, your ability

to work the room and meet people is limited. You'll meet only half the number of people, and those you do meet will think you are joined at the hip.

4. Develop a "rescue" signal so that you and your buddy can regroup to assess and restrategize, and help extricate one another from conversations that have gone on too long.

STRATEGY #3—
THE WHITE-KNUCKLE DRINKER
(AND OTHER ACCESSIBLE FOLK)

You're inside the room, and you and your buddy have decided it's time to split up. Where do you turn? Who do you talk to? You don't recognize a soul, and feel conspicuous standing alone. The temptation at this point is find a place near the wall and try to look like a paint chip.

Initiating conversation can be challenging. Remember, our mothers taught us NOT to talk to strangers. But we've remedied that. We also fear rejection, and perhaps suspect that we're not interesting, witty or attractive enough. But we've remedied those things, too. And because we are attending this reception in order to work the room, *we can't afford to be wallflowers*. It's time to step out there on our own, work up our courage, and do something.

What I do in this situation is look for the white-knuckle drinkers. If you want to manage the mingling at any event, look for people who are standing around with white knuckles. It doesn't matter whether their cup or glass contains a drink, wine, coffee or water—they are clutching it so tightly that their knuckles are white. They're scared to death and they are always alone.

These people usually welcome your conversation because you save them from anonymity. No one else is talking to them. If you walk up and start a conversation, you're doing a good deed and also moving *yourself* away from the wall.

SEIZE THE MOMENT. Make eye contact, smile, and say "Hello." Don't treat these people as losers. In most cases, they aren't. Maybe they are just shy or anxious. Make your conversation so fascinating that other people are drawn into your little group, and expand the circle.

Therese Godfrey, a Honolulu-based consultant and speaker, says, "When you care about other people's comfort more than your own, your clumsiness and self-consciousness go away."

Remember, the white-knuckle drinker is more uncomfortable than you are, and will be delighted with practically anything you have to say.

STRATEGY #4—NAMETAGS THAT PULL

While there are still mixed feelings about nametags, they are very important for business and social events. Nametags have some obvious benefits. Use them!

1. You can address a person by name, which is always preferable.

2. They provide information you can use to begin conversation (company, job title, location, area of specialty, etc.).

3. If you see "that familiar face" but aren't sure if the person is who you think he or she is, you can sneak a peek at the nametag.

At many trade shows, cocktail parties, and other events, nametags are provided. The person's name should be large and bold enough to be visible even if you are standing a few feet away. The company name is often a bit smaller, and you have to get closer to read it.

Many civic organizations and churches use nametags to encourage mingling. Sometimes the nametags are color-coded to distinguish members from guests or new members. "An unwritten rule is that members seek out guests and new members and make them feel welcome," according to Rick Enos, a senior member of The Guardsmen, a San Francisco civic organization. You might take a cue from this rule, and make yourself an unofficial greeter of guests and new members.

USING YOUR NAMETAG TO ADVANTAGE.

If you are asked to fill out your *own* nametag, you have some leeway in describing your position or specialty. This is a chance to identify yourself in an interesting way. Financial planner Fritz Brauner tells me that when he put the designation FINANCIAL PLANNER on his nametag at a business show, no one looked twice. But when he wrote MONEY beneath his name, he was approached by many interesting people who wanted to know what he did.

A sense of humor does help! At a Chamber of Commerce business social, one member had a nametag that caught my eye and made me laugh. Instead of writing his name, he had written NAMETAG. Corny, but we began a conversation quickly and easily.

PLACEMENT OF YOUR NAMETAG.

Always, always place the nametag on your right-hand side. When you extend your right hand for a handshake., the line of sight is to the other person's right side. If the nametag is placed on the left side and you sneak a peek away from the line of sight—you'll get caught! The idea is to make the nametag as visible as possible.

NO-NAMETAG EVENTS.

Nametags are not used at some business and many social events. (Only in California do you find them even at weddings!) At these events, you're on your own to introduce yourself to people and engage them in conversation. If they don't respond, all you can do is move away. . .with a renewed appreciation for the benefits of nametags.

THE FORGOTTEN NAME.

We all forget names from time to time, even the names of people who are important to us. People who must attend parties, benefits, conventions, fundraisers and reunions with humongous numbers of people can go into what I call "nomenclature overload!" Nametags will often prompt that "Bill Smith" that's just on the tip of your tongue.

We're all inclined to be hard on ourselves if we forget a name, but as one man said in an El Paso seminar, "I think we have unrealistic expectations of ourselves. We meet hundreds of people each week. Our parents may have met only ten new people in a week, and our grandparents perhaps only one! How can we expect to remember all those names?"

If you have forgotten a name or two, say so—with humor. Always state your own name when greeting another person. (They may have forgotten your name as well.) More often than not, they will reply in kind and the embarrassment of the forgotten name will be averted. We don't want to make people struggle with remembering our name. If you always state your name, you relieve the other person from "nomenclature overload" and will be remembered kindly.

STRATEGY #5—
GREAT OPENING LINES

The quest for the perfect opening line may be as old as humankind. Too often we lose an opportunity to meet someone because we spend precious time trying to think of the perfect opening line—and there is no such thing.

The good news is, there are a million perfect openers. What you say will depend upon who you are, the person to whom you are talking, the circumstances, the response you want to get, and what pops into your mind. It is far better to say *something* than to wait for the perfect clever remark. Even if what you say isn't going to change the world, don't lose the opportunity to begin a conversation.

Research now supports what expert minglers have always known: The best opening line of all may be a SMILE and a friendly "HI" or "HELLO!

One opener that's been suggested to me is, "Are you alone by choice or by chance?" That will give you a clue about how to proceed.

Some other good areas on which to comment are:

1. the facility
2. the food
3. the organization
4. the traffic and parking dilemma
5. the guest of honor
6. the charity/community that will benefit from the event

But what do you actually *say*? I always look to the MAGICAL THREE:

1. A STATEMENT.

Look around the room. Observe the situation. What is happening? Does there seem to be a good crowd? Do they seem to be enjoying themselves? Was the traffic or the parking difficult? What do these people have in common?

Observations about any of these things might be good conversation starters. Saying something humorous or unexpected is even better.

It's best to avoid negative comments. We don't want to give the impression of being whiners. Avoid statements like:

• "The food looks pathetic."
• "This hotel is far more run down that I had expected."

Go for upbeat, unusual observations that will pique people's interest.

2. A QUESTION.

The questions you ask should be relevant. Do your homework to find out about the group and the people who will be attending the event. Even if you don't know much about the organization, you can ask questions like:

- "Are you a member of this group?"
- "How would you suggest I become involved?"
- "How do you know the bride (honoree, groom, 'birthday boy,' anniversary couple, politician, etc.)?"

Questions should be open-ended enough to encourage a response. Here are some sample questions for various events:

Political Fundraiser:

- "What made you decide to support this candidate?"
- "How have you been involved in the campaign?"

Charity Benefit:

- "How did you get involved with the March of Dimes (Lung Association, etc.)?"

Professional Association Banquet:

- "Are you a member of this association?"
- "How have you been active in the organization?"

Neighbor's Daughter's Wedding:

- "Do you know the bride or groom?"
- "How did you meet him (or her)?"

Jogging Track:

- "How often do you run here?"
- "How does this compare to the other tracks you've run?"

I met my friend Rick Enos through a question I asked at a Chamber of Commerce After Hours at his Compadres Mexican Bar & Grill in San Francisco. I didn't realize that the guy carving the roast beef was the owner, but I asked this stranger which sauce he would recommend.

"That one is only Grey Poupon mustard, but this one is the Barbecue Sauce that is the house specialty—guaranteed to put sweat on your upper lip." Rick's sense of humor made me want to talk to him, and we became friends who are also part of one another's professional networks.

3. A PLEASANT SELF-REVELATION.

Disclosing something about yourself is a good way to establish your vulnerability and approachability, but there is a risk. Be careful not to reveal anything so personal that it burdens the listener.

* * *

Good Openers

- "I don't believe it took me forty-five minutes to get here and I was only three miles away!"
- "It never fails. I always manage to get teriyaki sauce on my tie. At least it highlights the design."
- "This food looks so good, I'm glad I forgot to eat lunch."

Self-disclosures should be generally positive. Some time ago, I attended a luncheon meeting for a professional association and said hello to one of the officers. When I asked how he was, he mentioned his separation. Then he elaborated on his teenage children's questions about his love life *and* his sex life. I realized he needed to talk to someone, but that meeting was neither the right time nor the right place...and I was not the right person.

Food is almost always a wonderful basis for communication. Grandma knew that food was a great conversation starter...that's one reason she made lots of it. It's no accident that meetings, get-togethers, social engagements and family affairs are often centered around a meal. When people come together over food, a certain amount of nurturing takes place—at least on the physical level, and often at the mental and professional levels as well.

Flirting

And while we're on the subject of great lines...What about flirting? What about the words, body language, facial expressions and glances that can find their way from a purely social situation to a business setting—or vice versa?

To some, flirting is a way of exchanging friendly banter, very much like small talk. Good natured, friendly banter is fine, and can be appropriate even in the office.

To others, flirting is a "come-on." It all depends on the flirter, the flirtee, and on what is actually being said and done.

Use caution with flirting in a business setting. One person's small talk is another person's come-on. Ask yourself if you want that deal, or that promotion, riding on what someone thinks of you as a business associate or as a potential date.

STRATEGY #6—
MOVING IN: BREAKING AND ENTERING

There is a difference between *including* yourself in other people's conversations, and *intruding* on them. Getting into a conversation that is already underway requires a dose of chutzpah, but also some sensitivity. Watch people's body language and listen to the tone of their conversation for clues.

One of my clients offers this advice for including without intruding:

1. Avoid approaching two people who look as though they are having an intense conversation. If they seem totally preoccupied, you can assume that they are flirting with some profound ideas or with one another.

2. Approach groups of three or more. Position yourself close to the group. Give only facial feedback to the

comments being made. When you feel yourself included, either by verbal acknowledgement or eye contact, you are free to join in the conversation.

3. Be open to others who "want in." When you see someone on the periphery of your conversational group, remember how uncomfortable you feel in that situation.

If you merely want to extend a greeting to someone in the conversation, you might say, "Excuse me for interrupting, but I wanted to say hello." Then move away. You may find that your interruption is a welcome relief and that you are invited to stay and chat.

What if someone interrupts *your* intense or important conversation? According to Dr. Geraldine Alpert, a psychologist in Marin County north of San Francisco, you can be both firm and gracious. Acknowledge the person politely and thank them for saying hello. Indicate that you need to finish this conversation but will catch up with them later. Then do so.

STRATEGY #7—
MOVING ON: EXTRICATING YOURSELF

Many of us feel uncomfortable with ending a conversation. Someone, somewhere, told us it was rude. Actually, the etiquette of cocktail parties is that we are supposed to circulate. No less an authority than Miss Manners suggests that we spend no more than eight to ten minutes with any one person. We have been invited so that we can mingle and meet the other attendees. It is an opportunity to circulate among peers, colleagues, potential clients, and to meet as many people as possible. The idea is NOT to engage in conversation with one person for the duration, although we sometimes do that because it can be easier.

GRACEFUL EXIT

How to make a graceful exit? I once found myself talking for twenty minutes to someone whose company I didn't find particularly pleasant or stimulating. When the colleague I was with asked why I had done that, I hemmed and hawed and said I hadn't wanted to be rude. "Susan," he said, "why didn't you just say 'EXCUSE ME'?"

That's all it takes. Even Miss Manners agrees. Her idea of a perfect exit line: "Excuse me, it's been lovely talking to you." I don't like to lie, so I occasionally find myself substituting, "Excuse me, it's been *interesting* talking to you." But the principle is the same.

To make your exit easier, wait until *you* have just finished a comment. Then smile and say, "Excuse me, it was nice meeting you." If it makes you feel more comfortable, you might add, "I think I see my boss (client, partner, spouse, mother-in-law)." The old "I need to freshen my drink" line has its drawbacks, because theoretically you should ask others if they would like their drinks freshened. Then you not only have to return, but you've bought them a drink.

Once you extricate yourself, visibly move to another part of the room. It underscores the fact that you really did have someone to see, or something to do, and that you didn't leave that person simply because you were bored.

Before you leave the event, be sure to thank the host or hostess. Even if it is a trade association luncheon rather than a social dinner party, someone is in charge and has spent time planning the food, the program, and all the details of the event. Seek that person out and thank him or her. Beware of the time-consuming, draining thirty-minute departure, in which you say goodbye over and over again, begin short conversations, say goodbye again, and slowly, painfully, inch yourself toward the door. Ronn Owens, a San Francisco radio talk show host, suggests that when you are ready to leave, LEAVE!

STRATEGIC DO'S AND DON'Ts

DO:

- Allow for serendipity. Be open to *all* the benefits you might encounter, not just those on which you've focused prior to the event.

- Follow up with those people you said you would call or contact, or with whom you said you would "do" lunch. If you don't intend to call, don't say you will.

- Bring your sense of humor. Not only will it attract people to you and make the evening more fun, it will get you through the faux-pas: forgetting names, spilling a drink, and most other potentially embarrassing moments. If you laugh first, you clear the air and become the likable person with lots of charm.

• Treat everyone nicely, whether or not their title impresses you. You never know. Looking for "Decision-Makers" may be a poor decision. They may be the most important person in the room, or they may be moving next week to positions that are not very impressive indeed.

• Dress appropriately. Let common sense prevail.

DON'T:

• Don't smoke cigars or pipes. Avoid cigarettes if you can. If you work a room with a cigarette, you may make an "ash" of yourself by dropping one on someone.

• Don't drink excessively. Even if it's 9 p.m., you are still "on the job" as long as associates and potential clients are around.

• Don't sit down. It's absolutely impossible to work a room on your TUSH!

REMINDERS

These seven strategies will help you work any room:

1. Enter the room with confidence, orient yourself, and look for people you either know or *want* to know.
2. Use the Buddy System.
3. Seek out the white knuckle drinkers and other people who will appreciate your interest and conversation.

4. Make the most of nametags.

5. Great opening lines come in a million forms. Just say "Hi" or "Hello." Anything will work if it's delivered with a smile and honest interest.

6. Don't be afraid to move in and join conversations already in progress.

7. Moving out of conversations is part of circulating through the room and meeting a variety of new people. Thank the host before you leave.

Chapter 8

WORKING THE WORDS: SIX KEYS TO LIVELY CONVERSATION

Chapter 8

You've prepared your presence and worked out your strategies for the event. You're in the room now and mingling with ease. You've even chosen someone you want to meet and introduced yourself with charm...and maybe a little chutzpah.

WHAT DO YOU SAY NEXT?

Even people who make wonderful self-introductions can be stymied by the next step...*making conversation.*

Initial impressions are based on our ability to communicate and converse. The trick is to do so with ease, interest, and energy. "Nothing is so contagious as enthusiasm; it moves stones, it charms brutes." This statement is attributed to Edward Bulwer-Lytton in *637 of the Best Things Anybody Ever Said.*

Sincere interest in people is the most important part of being a good conversationalist. If we are just waiting our turn to speak, or manipulating others into talking so we can get information, they will know it. We can listen to others not only with our ears, but with our eyes and our whole face to let them know we care about their responses, feelings and thoughts.

Be in the moment. Make those two minutes with each person memorable—by giving your undivided attention.

Your first topic of conversation with a new person probably will NOT be nuclear disarmament, abortion, or the possibility of world economic collapse—unless you are at an event organized around these issues.

Probably, you will talk small talk. Again, there is nothing small, phony or unimportant about verbal exchanges that work toward establishing common interests, or allow people to get to know one another better. I'm with Michael Korda: "There is nothing small about small talk."

The Six Keys to Lively Conversation will help both with initial small talk, and with the more in-depth discussions that may follow. They are designed to make conversation easier, and to give you something to say that is interesting and probe for interests you have in common with the other person.

Like everything else, good conversation requires planning!

KEY #1—
READ ONE NEWSPAPER A DAY

Reading a newspaper each day is a must! Some people balk at this suggestion—until they try it. This is not only the best way I know to build the knowledge bank from which to draw conversation, it can also be fun, entertaining, and even addictive! Once you start, it's hard to stop.

"Newstalk" is no substitute for reading the paper. Television and radio news programs can condense a war into fifteen seconds, a presidential election into thirty seconds. You simply can't get much insight into the issues in that amount of time.

People magazine is no substitute, and neither are other special interest magazines. Fascinating as these publications may be, they rarely deal in hard news and don't come out daily.

Why should a busy person with a multitude of demands on his or her time read a daily newspaper? Because a good conversationalist is well-read, well-versed and well-rounded. He or she knows what is going on in the world, and can talk about it. Reading the paper makes working any room infinitely more manageable.

Information is power. Building that "knowledge bank" lets us contribute to conversations with more ease and interest.

Do you have to be an expert on everything? Absolutely not. But you must be well-read enough to initiate or contribute to conversations. You need enough knowledge of general topics to pose intelligent questions.

Intelligent questions allow others to speak about their own areas of expertise and interest. They also give us the chance to learn from what other people says. Every event, meeting or party becomes an educational opportunity that provides us with additional information and resources to "bring to the next banquet."

TIPS FOR PERUSING THE PAPER

1. Start with your favorite section first—even if it is the comics. I start with Herb Caen's column in the

San Francisco Chronicle. There is usually at least one item that starts my day with a laugh.

2. If you are pressed for time and won't have a chance to read the whole paper until later, at least scan the headlines and first paragraphs. Fortunately, newspapers are written for busy people and so the major elements of any story—the who, what, where, when and how—are almost always covered in the first paragraph.

3. Read the business section—whether or not you find it particularly appealing at first. If you have a job or a career, you are in business and you need to know what is going on in the business world. You will be dealing with *other* people who are in business, and you need to know about their concerns.

    The business section isn't nearly as technical or intimidating as some people suspect. You don't have to be a venture capitalist to understand it. The business of newspapers is to *sell newspapers*, and they can't do this if they don't write things that regular people can comprehend and find interesting.

    Reading the business section gives you information that you can use to connect with people. One morning I read that the company for which I was doing a presentation that afternoon had just split its stock. It was important for me to refer to that information both in the presentation and in individual conversations. I was able to tap into something that excited those people and was already a topic of office discussion. Rather than distracting them from the stock split with my presentation, I was able to

incorporate it and make my talk much more interesting to them.

4. READ THE SPORTS PAGES! Even if you aren't an
    avid fan, you are sure to run *into* avid fans and this
    is a tremendous way to build rapport. Our goal in
    working a room is to make people feel comfortable
    with us and to create conversation. If other people
    are interested in the 49'ers, or the Cubs, or the Maple
    Leafs, then you are ahead of the game if you know
    something about the sport.

    You don't have to memorize batting averages for
    the last thirty years, but if the World Series is being
    played in the city where you are doing business, you
    should at least know what teams are involved and
    what is happening. It shows that you are well-
    rounded, and that you care about other people's
    interests. You may even become a fan yourself!

    Several years ago I called Jeff Waddle, who was
    then the editor of *Meeting Manager*, the journal of
    Meeting Planners International. We talked about
    some articles I hoped to place, and Jeff asked if I had
    been to Chicago for the MPI convention. I'd had
    prior commitments in San Francisco, so I said, "No,
    and it's too bad because I have a friend with seats in
    the bleachers at Wrigley Field."

    Eureka! I had hit paydirt because Jeff was a die-
    hard baseball fan and knew that, in Wrigley Field,
    the bleachers are the best seats in the house. He said
    he'd wanted to take in a game himself, but had been
    too busy with the convention. He was a Cincinnati

Reds fan, and we talked about baseball teams, parks, and Pete Rose for twenty minutes.

The result: Jeff published six of my articles in *Meeting Manager* over the next three years, and those articles have given me a lot of exposure in my industry. Meeting planners hire speakers. And although Jeff has changed jobs and is now a PR specialist in Cincinnati, we still keep in touch. What if my comment about the bleachers hadn't been so well received? Then I would have tried another tack. Chicago is my home town, and I would have made another comment about it or asked a question about the convention.

5. Don't forget the comics. 'Cathy' is one of my favorites, and has been the subject of many shared laughs. When a particular comic makes me think of someone I know, I often xerox it or tape it to a piece of my stationery and send it along— sometimes with a note. It's a good way to stay in touch, and humor is a wonderful way to connect.

6. Read the lifestyle section. Here you will find features, book excerpts and reviews, humor, commentary, fashion news, and articles on health, social issues, and...well, lifestyles. The lifestyle section is a wealth of information for your "knowledge bank," and much of it is perfect for starting and continuing conversations— statistics about stress, careers, divorce, back injuries, diets, commuting, etc.

* * *

KEY #2—
CLIP AND COLLECT

When I was in college, almost every letter from home contained a clipping. "The Relevant Article" was usually a letter to Ann Landers or Dear Abby from a broken-hearted mother whose daughter at college:

(Choose one)
a) did not write
b) did not call...unless there was a shortage of funds
c) did not plan to come home for a holiday
d) was not lavaliered or pinned
e) turned down dates with lovely, eligible fellows who were potential candidates for d) above

Imagine my dismay when I discovered that column-clipping is an *inheritied, genetic* quirk! The only consolation was that many of my colleagues had also inherited this chromosomal quirk, and it is a great conversation starter.

Jack Saunders, Director Stake Holder Contact District for Pacific Bell, admits to clipping. "I often send a copy of an article that relates to a conversation. It's a way of being remembered, while at the same time remembering and valuing someone you have met."

Saunders also collects humorous articles. He keeps them in a file, rereads them from time to time, and uses them as conversation starters. "I find that people will also laugh and respond...then the ice is broken."

Clipping and collecting articles and cartoons contributes to conversation—whether these clippings are poignant, satirical, relevant, or informative. Whether they press a hot button or, better yet, a funny bone, our own enthusiasm for whatever piqued our interest can be infectious.

KEY #3—
READ NEWSLETTERS,
PROFESSIONAL JOURNALS, AND MINUTES.

Sometimes we are invited to events sponsored by organizations with which we're not entirely familiar. Such events as charity fundraisers, political dinners, or clients' Christmas parties may require some special preparation. The best way to get a handle on the organization is to read its newsletter or professional journal.

These publications can be invaluable resources. If you invest the time to read them, you will be well compensated. You won't be an outsider; you will be familiar with the group and its people, and have all the information you need to ask questions and start conversations.

Should you recognize a member from a photo you saw in the newsletter or journal, you can bet that person will appreciate and welcome you.

The same is true of reading minutes of the organization's meetings. If you are attending a meeting of a new division or group, ask for the minutes for the past three months. You will impress people with your interest, get a better feel for what has been going on in the group, and be prepared to contribute interesting and pertinent information to conversations.

* * *

KEY #4—
TAKE NOTE AND TAKE NOTES

Other people's clever remarks and stories can be interesting, humorous, or poignant conversation starters. These statements or situations come from friends, associates, children, people on the street—practically anyone. They happen in the home, the office, at the health club or hair stylist—anywhere you have your ears open.

One advantage of these stories is that the hero or heroine is always someone else. Sometimes stories from two different people dovetail. My friend Lana Teplick, a Boston CPA, says of men, "Assume they are all married until proven otherwise." I shared this with another friend, Diane Bennett, and asked her how they might "prove otherwise." She replied, "Ask for their *home* numbers."

Another friend with whom I taught elementary school, Sylvia Cherezian, now has a 24-hour a day job raising two sons. One day when her son Charles was two, she cried in exasperation, "My God, I've given birth to a child whom I would *never* have allowed in my classroom!" I share that comment with colleagues who mention that they have children and the conversation flows.

In order to use these comments and situations as conversation starters, we have to *remember* them. Some people write them down in a journal each evening; others carry a small spiral notebook to jot them down. Even the most unforgettable line or story can get lost if we don't take the time to record it somewhere.

I often share the best piece of advice I received from my personal and professional mentor, Joyce Siegel: "Do not spend your time with anyone whom, after you leave, you waste one minute thinking about what they meant by what was said."

KEY #5—
USE HUMOR (SURELY YOU JEST)

Humor has a special way of bringing people together. It can establish rapport and warmth among people. It's a unique and magical elixir that can even heal the body.

Both management and medical research support the value of humor. Laughter is good for your health, according to Dr. William Fry of Stanford Medical School. "Laughter works by stimulating the brain to produce hormones that help ease pain. It also stimulates the endocrine system, which may relieve symptoms of disease. Laughter can also help feelings of depression," Dr. Fry says.

You don't have to be a standup comic to use humor. Humor can be defined in two ways. First, it is the quality of being funny, and second, it is the ability to perceive, enjoy or express something funny.

The right sentence or phrase at the right moment can save a negotiation or a board meeting. But humor should be used judiciously, because it can offend as well as delight. I'm usually wary when I hear the phrase, "Did you hear the one about the...?"

* * *

HUMOR DO'S AND DON'T'S

DO:

- Practice your stories and punchlines. I once practiced my opening story for a presentation seventeen times before the timing was right.
- Watch comedies, both on television and at the movies, and read books about humor. I watch *Golden Girls* with a paper and pencil by my side and always attribute the funny line to the correct Golden Girl.
- Use the "A.T.& T." rule to check any story or joke. Is it Appropriate? Is it Tasteful? Is it Timely?
- Laugh at yourself: it is a trait of people who take risks. Some of the best stories are those you tell on yourself.

DON'T:

- "Don't tell jokes if you don't tell them well, " advises Patricia Fripp, internationally acclaimed professional speaker.
- Don't put people down. "Roasting" can create a slow burn—one that can backfire.
- Don't use humor that is racist, sexist, homophobic, or "humor" that slurs religion, ethnic origin, or disability.
- Don't be afraid to let go and laugh. It's good for your health and makes working the room a lot more enjoyable.

* * *

KEY #6—
LISTEN ACTIVELY, NOT PASSIVELY

As a raconteur and "talker," I have always been sensitive to the criticism about talkers. But research shows that just because a person is a good "talker" doesn't mean he or she is not also a good "listener."

All of us need to be good listeners, and that means more than staring into someone's eyes while he or she talks—and you plan tomorrow's meeting or rethink the movie you saw last night.

Active listening means *hearing* what people say, concentrating on them and their words, and then responding. When we really concentrate on that one person and are in the moment, we improve our chances of remembering both the person and the conversation.

In the "How to Work a Room" seminar, people practice role-playing as "talkers" and "listeners." Thousands of "talkers" have said that the most important behaviors of active listening, the things that most encouraged them to talk, were what I call The Significant Seven:

1. Eye contact
2. Nodding
3. Smiling and/or laughing
4. Asking relevant questions that indicate interest
5. Making statements that reflect similar situations
6. Facial expressions
7. Body language that is open and receptive

If we are conscious of listening actively, our conversational skills will improve. Working a room will be less work and more fun. Conversation may be a dying art, but with preparation and interest, we can revive it.

REMINDERS

It takes some planning and attention to make yourself an effective conversationalist. But the planning itself can be fun. Not only will you be gathering information, but also learning interesting facts (If it's not, why waste the file space?) and the reward will be that making conversation becomes easier and more pleasant.

Remember: Practice the Six Keys to Lively Conversation:

1. Read one newspaper a day
2. Clip and collect
3. Read newsletters, professional journals, and minutes
4. Take note and take notes
5. Use humor (Surely you jest)
6. Listen actively

Chapter 9

WORKING THE RULES OF ETIQUETTE: WHEN POLITE IS NOT ENOUGH

Chapter 9

Good manners are good business.

Mention the terms "etiquette" or "good manners" to entrepreneurs and the most boring or vacuous meeting becomes highly charged. Why would such old fashioned terms create that lively interest? One reason is that manners and etiquette seem to be disappearing.

Many people are too "busy" or preoccupied with "more important things" to practice common courtesies— responding to R.S.V.P.'s, extending a "thank you," making good introductions, and treating others with courtesy and respect. Yet bad manners can be deadly...both to the reputation and to the bottom line. It's not nice to hurt peoples' feelings, and it's not good business practice, either.

The opposite is true as well. "If you have a great product, a commitment to service, and treat your customers and employees with common courtesy, the market share will take care of itself," says Tom Peters, consultant, speaker, and co-author of *In Search of Excellence*.

How are we *supposed* to behave at a party, reception or convention? The answer: VERY WELL!

But what is "behaving well?" The expectations are much the same as those that parents and teachers have of children:

1. Know the rules
2. Observe the rules
3. Do so graciously

If you don't already know the rules of formal etiquette and business etiquette, it's wise to learn them. Many good references are available in book stores and libraries.

The problem is, so many of the rules have changed that even people who were taught various "white glove" schools of etiquette often don't have any idea what they're doing. Experts are scrambling to write books on "new etiquette," "business etiquette," "sexual etiquette," "teen etiquette," you name it! Clearly, things have changed.

ETIQUETTE AND MANNERS

Etiquette is defined as the usages and rules for behavior in polite society, official or professional life. Certain basic rules are still accepted as the norm, and it behooves us to know both the *old* etiquette and the *new* etiquette.

But knowing the rules of etiquette is not enough. What we're really after is manners—that wonderful combination of courtesy, caring, and common sense.

There is a difference between knowing the rules of etiquette and being a person of manners. Some people follow every rule of etiquette, but have a manner that is rude or patronizing.

A Washington hostess noticed that one of her guests used the wrong fork at a formal dinner, and pointed out this error to him in front of the other guests. She knew the proper etiquette, but showed a lack of good manners. Why? People with good manners don't embarrass others.

In contrast, when Lady Astor's guest picked up the wrong fork, she picked up the wrong fork, too, so that he wouldn't be embarrassed.

Noah Griffin, San Francisco radio talk show host and PR specialist, says that "people with manners are those who treat others in such a way that everyone is comfortable with them."

People with good manners also treat others with respect. Knowing the rules is one thing; caring about people and treating them with consideration is something else.

Bob Beck is executive vice president of Corporate Human Resources for the Bank of America. After a talk, he was asked whom he credited with giving him the most help in his career. Members of the audience edged forward in their seats to learn the name of this important mentor. "My mother," Bob said. "She not only taught me that I could do whatever I tried, but also how to treat people *courteously*."

Courtesy is the cornerstone of good manners. According to my *Standard Collegiate Dictionary*, "to be courteous is to be polite while having a warmer regard for the feelings and dignity of others."

If people are comfortable with us, our presence at any event will be valued. And we will be remembered. . .for the right reasons.

* * *

MANNERS MAVENS

The bad news is that the rules have changed...and continue to change.

The good news is that it's easy to get help. The changing rules of etiquette have spawned a whole new industry. Books, columns, seminars, and even software programs on etiquette are readily available. There is a great demand for expert consultants who can show us the acceptable conventions for social and business behavior, because people *want to know*.

Miss Manners (to whom you may only write in blue or blue-black ink—never peacock blue) has written several books and has a syndicated column. Letitia Baldrige, former social secretary to Jackie Kennedy, has written both *Letitia Baldrige's Complete Guide to Executive Manners* and a revised edition of *Amy Vanderbilt Complete Book of Etiquette*. There is a plethora of practical guides.

Baldridge claims that manners are 99% common sense and 1% kindness.

THE R.S.V.P.

R.S.V.P. stands for "Repondez s'il vous plait." This translates from the French as "Respond if you please." (And if you don't, you may not get invited again—at least to my house.)

A social invitation requires a response. That's all there is to it. To compensate for a general deterioration in etiquette, response cards are often included in invitations.

* * *

R.S.V.P. FOR BUSINESS

R.S.V.P.s for business events, meetings, and association luncheons are a bit different. The expectation is that you will pre-register and pre-pay, or call in a reservation. And you are expected to attend if you reserve! You generally do not have to call to say you won't be able to attend unless you've already responded and committed to being there.

It's not nice to be a "drop-in." I have attended many luncheons where too many "busy" people (*much* too busy to bother calling in a reservation) showed up at the door at the last minute. The food count was thrown way off balance— and so was the luncheon's chairperson! Leftovers for an army (or worse, a shortage of shrimp puffs) is every host's nightmare.

If you find out at the last minute that you'll be able to attend after all, at least call the morning of the event to let them know you're coming.

To R.S.V.P. shows good manners, consideration, breeding and respect.

INTRODUCTIONS

Many people feel awkward about introductions because they remember being taught that there was one right way to do it—and they can't remember what that one right way is. So they stand there, with two people whom they want to introduce, stammering, Uh...Jim, meet Susan...uh, no...Susan, Jim. My friend...uh..." Much of the warmth goes out of an introduction when we don't feel comfortable.

It helps if there is a reception line. If you see one, head directly for it and introduce yourself to the host. Give some information about yourself that he or she can pass on as you are introduced to the next person in line. If there is no reception line, take a deep breath and rely on the strategies we've discussed. If you spot people with "host" badges, introduce yourself to them and hope that they will introduce you around.

Letitia Baldrige makes introductions very simple in her *Complete Guide to Executive Manners*. She says that the most important thing to remember about introducing people is *to do it*, even if you forget names, get confused, or blank out on the proper procedure. Introducing people is one of the most important acts in business life..."

She offers five logical guidelines:

1. Introduce a younger person *to* an older person.
2. Introduce a peer in your own company *to* a peer in another company.
3. Introduce a nonofficial person *to* an official person.
4. Introduce a junior executive *to* a senior executive.
5. Introduce a fellow executive *to* a customer or client.

The idea is always to introduce the "less important" person to the "more important" person. (We know these people aren't really less or more important on a human level, but we're dealing here with arbitrary societal conventions.)

Baldrige offers these examples:

- "Mr. Cogswell, I'd like to present my daughter Cynthia. Cynthia, this is Mr. Gregory Cogswell, the president of our company."
- "Mr. and Mrs. Johnson, I'd like to introduce to you a fellow executive from Standard Oil, Timothy Greet."

"Tim, this is Mr. and Mrs. Oleg Johnson, good friends of my parents."

About using people's titles, she says, "When introducing people of equal standing, you do not have to use a title unless you are introducing an older person, a professional, or someone with official rank." In other words, you might use the "titles" of Dr. James, Senator Parker, Reverend Smith, or Rabbi Cohen—but the two new vice presidents might be simply Amanda Randall and Howard Waller.

When introducing a public official, use his or her title even if he or she no longer holds the position. You would say either "Mayor Feinstein" or "former Mayor Feinstein; "President Nixon" or "former President Nixon."

Proper etiquette is important in introductions, but we shouldn't become such slaves to it that we lose our warmth or our humor. The most important thing is that people know you *want* them to meet one another. When in doubt, just give the names and some indication of who the people are and what they might have in common.

NAMING NAMES

People like to be remembered...by name. But it's not easy to remember everyone, particularly if we meet a lot of people.

The classic Name Nightmare...You are at a reception for a local charity, attended by about two hundred people and held in the ballroom of a local hotel. A man approaches you and says, "Craig, it's so good to see you again!"

Your mind races, your heart pounds, a bead of perspiration forms on your brow. You don't have a clue who this person is.

What to do? Pretend you don't see or hear him, turn, and make a hundred-yard dash across the room? Duck under the buffet table? Beat your breast and throw yourself on his mercy?

Obviously not. The best solution is to tell the truth. . . preferably with some humor. You might try:

- "Forgive me. Since I've turned forty, I barely remember my own name." (This is what I've been saying since the Big Four O.)

- Please, help me out. I've just gone blank. . . it's genetic (or, it's been a hectic day, etc.)."

Who is going to say, "No, I want to watch you squirm until you remember my name?

By the same token, don't let people squirm to remember *your* name or who you are. State your name clearly, immediately, and with energy. Give the other person some idea of who you are or how you may have met. Mani Costa, Director of the Myrtle Beach Convention Center, tells people that he works for the city. "That allows the other person to ask me a question and feel good about expanding our conversation."

Memory expert Dr. Joan Minninger offers some tips for remembering names. The first is to *decide to remember.* She recommends that we say our name, and repeat the other person's name, while shaking hands—because this physical gesture makes for kinesthetic reinforcement. Looking for an unusual physical characteristic and focusing on it also helps connect the name with the face.

And finally, for those of us who did not grow up in California (where everyone is called by his or her first name), there is the problem of what to *call* people. Do we use the first name, the "Mr., Mrs., or Ms." form, or the formal title.

Option #1: Use the formal title (Dr. Jones, Ms. Smith, Lt. Wright, Supervisor Benson). People who want you to call you by their first names will invite you to do so. 'Please call me Jim.' If they don't offer the first name, stick to the title.

Option #2: Ask. Do you prefer to be called Dr. Brown?"

Congressman Joseph Kennedy II (D-Massachusetts) fielded this issue gracefully at a San Francisco fundraiser. After he had finished his remarks and asked for questions, one of the participants addressed him as "Mr. Kennedy." (In fact, it should have been Representative or Congressman Kennedy.) Kennedy laughed and said, "Oh, oh. When you call me that, I *know* I'm in trouble! Please, call me Joe."

THANK YOU'S

Not everyone writes thank you notes these days, but it is an extremely gracious gesture and one that is appreciated by every host or hostess. Think of how you would feel if you'd had ten people to dinner. Wouldn't it be nice to get a note from someone thanking you for all you'd done to make the evening pleasant?

Dr. Vera Pitts, a professor at a California State University points out, "If I take the time to plan the menu, shop, clean the house, cook, serve the dinner, and clean up, that may take four to six hours! My guest certainly has a few moments to write a note or card to say thank you."

Strict etiquette may no longer require thank you notes for every event, but they are good manners.

To write, to type, or to word process? Handwritten notes are quickly becoming a lost art, and some people complain that it takes too much time to write thank you notes by hand. But most "manners mavens" agree that the handwritten note is more valued. It reflects personal care, thought, and time expended.

At a seminar for a major public accounting firm in the South, one of the young fast-track CPA's pointed out that he could connect with many more people using computer-generated notes.

True, but a senior partner and true Southern gentleman suggested, "While everyone else is being computer efficient with their notes, why don't we take the time, personalize the notes and really distinguish ourselves?"

Tom Peters always responds to his mail with brief handwritten notes. "Busy" is not the issue. Tom Peters is far busier than most people who claim they don't have the time to write notes.

If you just can't bring yourself to write, there is a "surrogate communicator." The suggestion comes from Jim Delahunty, former Hallmark sales rep and current card shop owner. "We even help customers find the 'right' card."

MISCELLANEOUS MANNERS (TWO TIPS)

1. People expect that we will "bring something to the banquet." That means, at the very least, energy, enthusiasm, conversation, information, and humor. Approach people with a smile, a handshake and an open, upbeat greeting. And look them in the eye. Invite people into your conversations once they get started.

2. Don't let your good time go up in smoke. Smoking is a burning issue in the 80's and will be in the 90's. We may have the legal right to smoke in most places, but it is offensive to many people and may not be prudent.

REMINDERS

It's important to consult the "manners mavens" to keep abreast of changing patterns in etiquette, but even more important to be a person of manners—one who genuinely cares about other people and makes an effort to make them feel comfortable. Manners are a combination of common sense and kindness.

Do the gracious thing, the thing you would like done if you were in the other person's place—whether you are responding to invitations, making introductions, or extending a "thank you."

The bottom line: Be nice, and be thoughtful.

GO!

Chapter 10

WORKING THE COCKTAIL PARTY WITH PLEASURE, PURPOSE AND PANACHE

Chapter 10

You're all set. You've reviewed the roadblocks and applied the remedies. You've focused in on the potential benefits and prepared both your presence and your strategies. You are ready to converse with just the right balance of chutzpah and charm, and you know your manners as well as your etiquette.

Now it's time to take that wealth of knowledge and that enthusiasm for mingling out into the world. In the next few chapters, we will focus on four of the "rooms" that are now at your feet: the cocktail party, the reunion, the trade show, and...yes, the world!

The cocktail party is here to stay as a business and social function. Surviving them is good; making the most of them and having a good time in the process is even better!

Cocktail parties are gatherings of about two hours where drinks and finger food are served and guests are expected to stand and to circulate. There are three basic types of cocktail party:

1. Social
2. Business
3. Fundraiser (charitable, civic, political, etc.)

THE COCKTAIL PARTY—SOCIAL

The social cocktail party is making a comeback. It never really disappeared, but it is more popular now than ever because, according to Martha Stewart, entertainment columnist for the *San Francisco Chronicle*, it is a "simpler process than a sit-down dinner and can reciprocate social obligations." You can return invitations without hiring a staff of twenty or spending a week making food.

Heavy sit-down dinners are also less common because we have become a nation of "grazers." We want a sliver of this and a taste of that. We love to nibble and nosh, to experiment and combine different kinds of foods.

The social cocktail party may have a theme or "occasion" based on holidays or events. It might celebrate an engagement, a housewarming, Halloween, Valentine's Day, Christmas, or simply that the host/hostess felt like having a party and inviting his or her friends to meet one another.

If there is a written invitation, you will probably be asked to R.S.V.P. and you must definitely do so. If your hosts request a specific attire (costumes, casual, black tie optional, etc.), adhere to it. It is their party, and they have put some effort into planning it. Don't let them be the only ones in the room wearing gorilla suits or black tie.

Unless someone buttonholes you immediately after you walk in the door, your first stop will be the hosts. It is their job to meet, greet, and introduce you to others. Good hosts always have a vignette or two about each guest that make introductions easier and more interesting.

After you have begun to meet people, remember that Miss Manners stresses *mingling* and *circulating*. The hosts have invited you so that you can meet their other friends. It's rude to latch on to one person and sit in the corner with that person for the rest of the evening.

A TIP TO HOSTS: Placing the food and beverages at different locations around the room encourages guests to circulate.

At the social cocktail party, you can always fall back on "How do you know Bob (the host)?" for a conversation starter.

Even though the party may be purely social, you, of course never leave home without your business cards and so you will have a good supply of them with you. You might meet your biggest client of the year, your new best friend, or someone who can coach your daughter's soccer team.

Even if the encounter is completely social—or perhaps even romantic—business cards are a better way to exchange information than scrawling phone numbers on wine-soaked napkins with filthy old golf pencils, or thrashing around in your purse or wallet for deposit slips. Is this the way you want the relationship to begin?

Remember: Thank the hosts before you leave.

THE COCKTAIL PARTY—BUSINESS

Business cocktail parties come in several varieties:

1. The No-Host reception before the professional association meeting

2. The office party, which may celebrate anything from the company's anniversary to a holiday

3. The business social, which is often sponsored by the Chamber of Commerce, the Convention and Visitors Bureau or some other civic organization.

THE NO-HOST RECEPTION

The no-host reception is usually forty-five minutes to an hour long and precedes a business luncheon or dinner meeting. You register for the reception when you register for the meeting, and there is generally a no-host bar.

This is a time for members to reconnect with one another, and to meet new people who have been brought as guests. It is also an opportunity for you to bring guests who might be interested in joining the association. If you are a guest, it is a time for you to find out about the organization. For both members and guests, it is a great opportunity to interact.

There is usually no official host at these events, but there is often a greeting committee. Introduce yourself to someone on the committee. They should find at least one other person to whom they can introduce you, and then you're on your own. Pull out your bag of tricks, warm up your smile, and begin to work the room!

Conversation starters are everywhere at these events. If you are a guest, you can ask questions about the organization and the various ways of participating. If you are already a member, this is a time to renew acquaintances and meet new people in your field. You will also want to extend yourself to guests and new members so that they feel more comfortable and welcome.

Remember. . .the focus here is BUSINESS—with a social flair, to be sure—but it's still important to do your homework and work the room so that you make new contacts and strengthen old ones. This kind of cocktail reception is usually followed by a sit-down meal, a program, and announcements. So even when the reception is over, you have another opportunity to meet the people during the meal.

THE MEAL: SIT DOWN, YOU'RE ROCKING THE BOAT!

The first rule: Do *not* sit with people you know. If you just wanted to spend time with your friends, you could have gone out for a pizza. This is a chance to meet 7–9 new people, all of whom have something in common with you. Don't miss the opportunity!

Introduce yourself to the group at the table and ask the others to do the same. This is a risk, but the rewards are great. The person you really want to talk to could be sitting on the other side of the table, rather than next to you. If you hadn't gone around the table and introduced yourselves, you might never have known that he was there. After the meal is over, there will be time for a more private conversation, and you will have him pinpointed.

The dress for these occasions is usually what you would wear to the office, but it can get a bit tricky around the holidays. Several years ago I attended the holiday party of a local professional association. I was wearing a dressy suit; one of the other women wore a strapless long gown. One of us was dressed inappropriately. I never figured out which one. When in doubt, make some subtle inquiries.

THE OFFICE PARTY

The office party is a different kind of animal from the no-host reception before a professional association meeting. It *is business*, despite the trappings that may confuse us—music, formal invitations, dancing, drinking, etc.

If clients are in attendance, you are also a host—whether or not you own the company.

Remember the cautions about alcohol consumption, appropriateness of conversation and humor, and the need for business greeting etiquette even if your co-workers have forgotten them and are running around the typing pool with lampshades on their heads. That's no way to work a room.

The Office Christmas Party is notorious for this type of behavior. I've heard many stories of inebriation, sickness, flirtations, and dalliances that have lost promotions and even jobs. Even the Office Christmas Party is business. Go to have a good time in the spirit of the holiday season, but don't exceed the bounds of taste or reason.

That doesn't mean standing in the corner acting like the original wet blanket. Dr. Luann Lindquist tells the story of attending the staff dinner dance for a local hospital and noticing that one of the men was not dancing with his girlfriend. She was curious and asked him why he was not out on the dance floor. His reply was interesting. "These people are my colleagues; I work with them and our relationship is professional. I do not want them to have an image of me boogeying."

Dancing and relaxing are definitely *not* out of line. This is a good chance to chat with colleagues in a less pressured setting. It may also be a great time to give kudos to those who have helped you, or who have been particularly encouraging or supportive.

Spouses who attend office parties should be treated as real people, individuals in their own right and not just appendages of the person who works with you. It's not easy being a spouse at an office party, and the person who makes an effort to meet and chat with spouses is always appreciated. Try to find out what the spouse's interests are instead of talking only about your colleague and the work you share.

THE BUSINESS SOCIAL

The business social is often called the "After Hours" and it has become a staple of many Chambers of Commerce and other civic organizations. It is an event made to order for creating visibility and meeting other business people in your city.

These functions are usually held about once a month and are open to members and their guests. People who attend them have in common:

1. Membership in the organization

2. Business interest in the community.

That represents a wide range of conversation starters!

Research shows that it is easier to remember a person's profession than it is to remember his or her name. At the business social, people usually talk about what they *do*. This is no accident. The business social is one of the best forms of free advertising anywhere—if you know how to work the room. I faithfully attended my San Francisco Chamber of Commerce business socials and actually do much of my "hands on" research at these events. I've met people at these events who have become dear friends as well as valued associates. I've dramatically increased my base of referrals—and I've gained more visibility than I could possibly afford through advertising.

The business social is not usually a place to finalize deals or sign contracts; it's a place to meet people, get to know them better, and discover what you have in common and how you might support one another—even if it is "only" moral support. It's an opportunity to establish rapport.

People do business with people they know, like and trust. Again, etiquette, manners and courtesy are the keys.

Gayle Wilhelm, manager of the San Francisco Chamber of Commerce Small Business Division, says, "The people who get the most out of business events have three traits I've observed. 1) They *want* to be there; 2) They are prepared... with cards; and 3) They have a clear idea of who they want to meet. But there is a special quality of those who work an event well that I feel is most exemplified by my own father: graciousness. My dad, Robert Wilhelm, managing director of the Westin St. Francis Hotel, comes to events as himself and his company. And he treats *everyone* with importance!"

No matter how clear your focus, the impression you create depends on your ability to communicate a genuine caring and a sincere generosity of spirit.

THE FUNDRAISER—YOUR MONEY, OR...

The third type of cocktail party is the fundraiser. Its purpose is to benefit a charity or community organization. Or it may be to "honor" a politician or political hopeful by raising funds for the campaign coffers.

Carl La Mell is the Executive Director of the Victor Neumann Association and must attend many of these events. Due in large part to his style of fundraising and gathering support, the Association has expanded from a base of $500,000 to a base of $3.5 million. He says, "After working a full day, I rarely *want* to go to a cocktail party or reception. But once I am there, I am ready to do my job *and* have a good time."

When *we* are having a good time, our enthusiasm generates enthusiasm in others. They want to be around us, and to do business with us.

La Mell's advice for working fundraisers:

1. Know who you have to see.
2. Make sure they *do not* know that it's your goal to see them.
3. Do not talk about business, make the connection, set rapport and make sure they know who you are.
4. Do not overstay your welcome. You cannot monopolize any one person.
5. Depending on the response to you, get the business card.
6. Follow up!

"Yes, once you do your homework, you can target the room," La Mell says. "But, absolutely *never* ignore people. Each individual is a potential connection, and you have to treat everyone with regard."

Again—it's authentic interest and gracious manners that get the response.

La Mell's point is echoed by Bob Johnson and Bill Racek, General Manager and Senior Vice-President of the Louisiana Superdome: "Make the connection and do not belabor your point. Following up in a social way is soft sell and establishes rapport."

PARTY POLITICS

At a political fundraiser, everyone has to donate money in order to attend. The reasons for donating money to a candidate are as varied as the number of people in attendance, but everyone has in common an interest in the candidate or the organization's success.

Often there is Big Name Entertainment...but the real "draw" is a chance to meet the candidate or office holder. If the politician is working the room properly and you are not hanging out behind the curtains, *you should get that chance.* Make the most of it. Put yourself forward in a gracious way, introduce yourself, and say something memorable...and brief. The politician wants to meet and connect with you, but he or she may need to do the same with hundreds of people in only a few hours. A short, unusual quip will make you stand out in the sea of faces.

We assume that all politicians have mastered the art of working a room. After all, the phrase "working a room" came to us from politics. But this isn't always the case. Politicians have all the same roadblocks we do. It's just that their very survival depends on remedying those roadblocks. And they wouldn't be where they are if they hadn't had some success in doing so.

Can you imagine a politician who heeded Mother's Dire Warning: "Don't talk to strangers?" That's a politician who can barely pay for his meal, let alone buy television advertising! And how would you like to be one of that politician's constituents? Until you'd been properly introduced, you couldn't even tell him about the pothole on your street.

John Molinari, member of the San Francisco Board of Supervisors and 1987 candidate for Mayor, believes that there are two types of fundraising events: those that are held for you, and those that are held for a candidate for another office or to raise money for a community organization (both of which may be attended by your constituents).

"The fundraiser in my honor was much easier because people who attended were supportive," he says. "The issue for me is balancing two to four conversations at once with people that want several words *alone* with you. I believed I owed each person that time and tried to do just that. And it was tough. The event that honors someone else is different. You have to judge the event and the people and not overstep your bounds. It is poor campaign form to get up and move from table to table when you are not the honoree. We need to exhibit manners and respect for protocol and for other people."

THE KENNEDY CHARISMA... PLUS!

I have watched Congressman Joseph Kennedy of Massachusetts work a room, and it is a remarkable experience. He was the featured speaker at a foundation fundraiser, but the way he worked the room is a lesson to all of us— whether we are being honored or simply attending the event.

Before the speech, he went around to each table and spoke to every single person at the event. He wasn't just "pumping flesh"; he was *connecting* with each person. He smiled, he looked into their eyes, he exuded warmth, he *touched* people, he was funny. He had something to say to everyone and he listened when they talked, hearing what they said and responding appropriately. He laughed. When he talked to me, he wasn't looking somewhere over my shoulder to see who else was in the room. It's impossible to fake charisma. The interest, the warmth, the sparkle, and the humor have to be real or people know it—especially under the glare of the spotlight, where Kennedy lives. Joe Kennedy's charisma has nothing to do with being handsome. It has to do with his ability to convey genuine pleasure in meeting and talking with people, and his ability to respond to them as individuals and to generate warmth and enthusiasm in everyone around him.

H. Lee Evans, a San Francisco attorney, met Kennedy at another event and told me, "He was incredible. So many politicians I've supported expect you to approach *them*. Joe Kennedy walked over to us, extended his hand and introduced himself. He asked about us and told some stories about a recent trip to Ireland. As I was leaving, he came over and said, 'Lee, thanks for coming!' I was impressed...and I'm hosting a fundraiser for him in a couple months."

What can we learn from this master of working a room? Beyond the obvious charmers—eye contact, smiling, touching, shaking hands, humor, speaking and listening to each individual, laughing—there was a special warmth and sense of caring about Joe Kennedy because *he looked like he was having a fantastic time himself*. Connecting with people didn't appear to be a chore for him; it appeared to be a joy. It makes us happy when we bring joy to other people. All of us at that fundraiser felt like we were bringing joy to Joe Kennedy that night...and he gave us joy in return.

When we honestly enjoy other people's company, we hardly have to think about how to work a room. All the "right" things come naturally, because we *want* to make people feel comfortable and cared for. They respond to that, and to us.

* * *

REMINDERS

The cocktail party—social, business, or fundraiser—is a perfect opportunity to meet new friends and new contacts, and to reconnect with familiar faces. Never forget your business cards, your smile, nor your sense of humor. Go to have a good time, enjoy the people, and remember your focus.

Chapter 11

WORKING THE REUNION: REELING IN REALITY

EACH FITNESS PROGRAM IS DE-SIGNED FOR THE GOALS OF THE INDIVIDUAL.... THIS WOMAN IS PREPARING TO GET INTO WHITE STRETCH PANTS IN AUGUST.

THIGH MACHINE.

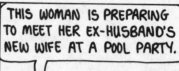

THIS WOMAN IS PREPARING TO MEET HER EX-HUSBAND'S NEW WIFE AT A POOL PARTY.

BUST MACHINE

THIGH, BUST, REAR, WAIST & ARM MACHINE

OLYMPIC TRIALS?

HIGH SCHOOL REUNION.

7-23

Chapter 11

If you doubt that reunions are a major cause of weight loss in America, just ask anyone who has ever attended one. My twentieth high school reunion in Chicago prompted three weeks of starvation and many questions.

Why would any busy person leave her business and home for days to reconnect with the past? Why would any sane person fly 2,000 miles to see high school classmates? My motive for going was a combination of curiosity, friendship, business and lots of warm feelings for a very nice group of "kids."

It was worth every moment of fear and trepidation. I had a terrific time, reconnected with old friends, and even did some good business.

JUST GO!

At a reunion, the room is *not* filled with strangers! For some, this is a plus. You definitely have something in common with your old classmates—even if it's a dreaded algebra teacher of days gone by.

For others, having a history with these people is a drawback. The invitation to the reunion may unearth old pains and insecurities. (Who among us was truly secure and serene at age seventeen)? It may prompt fear about comparisons—professional, social, marital, and monetary. And always, always, there is the Pound Problem—for men as well as women. Gloria Steinem tells the story of her Smith reunion, and says that no one was as concerned about professional success, marital bliss, children, or who had found the meaning of life as they were about WEIGHT. The first thing everyone said to her was, "You're so THIN!"

The thought of voluntarily returning to celebrate the days of yesteryear can be chilling! Will it be too disillusioning to see the football hero with a beer belly and a balding pate? Or to discover that cheerleaders have *thighs*?

Will everyone want to probe your personal life, picking for imperfections? Will they want to see your last six bank statements? Hear all about your first date after the divorce?

Probably not. The fact is, people are clamoring to reunions. One reason is that Baby Boomers are reaching the age for twenty- and twenty-five-year reunions. Another reason is that, despite all the terrible trepidations and worst fears, despite the months of dieting and starvation and aerobics, despite the foreboding about seeing the person with whom you did "everything but," and despite the time and expense that is usually involved—most people have a fantastic time at their reunions and would do it again tomorrow!

The reunion is a formal social event with a long history, and it is more popular today than ever. This is evidenced by the proliferation of companies created just to research, plan, and produce reunions. Shell and Judy Norris of Class Reunion, Inc. in Skokie, Illinois, have established the National Association of Reunion Planners as an umbrella organization for their colleagues.

Across the country, people are overcoming the usual reunion neuroses—what to wear, what to weigh, what to do, what to say—and flocking to their reunions. Judy Markey, syndicated columnist for the *Chicago Sun Times* and author of *How to Survive Your High School Reunion And Other Mid-Life Crises*, recommends that we "abandon all that knee-jerk negativism, and just GO. Here's why. Because sullen, difficult adolescents actually metamorphose into wonderful adults. You'll be in a veritable roomful of you're-not-getting-older-you're-getting-betters."

Besides, now that you know how to work a room, you may come away with a whole new group of friends, people whose presence is fresh and exciting but who also knew you "when."

Last but certainly not least, you may discover some wonderful business contacts among your old gym or geography buddies.

* * *

REUNION REFERRALS

My primary purpose in attending my reunion was to reconnect with old friends and, frankly, to see what had become of people since we last saw one another twenty years ago.

But I also saw it as a business opportunity. As long as I was going back to Chicago, I scheduled some appointments there. I sent letters to meeting planners in Chicago about ten days before the reunion. The result: I was hired by the American College of Surgeons to speak in 1987 based on the 1984 reunion contact.

Business opportunities aren't limited to your former classmates. If you are traveling to your home town, give some thought to other potential contacts there.

I took business cards with me to the reunion. Even if you only intend to socialize, it is far better to exchange cards than to write your address or phone number on a used napkin. It's important not to be consumed by the potential business aspects of a reunion or you risk creating the impression of a "hard sell," but reunions are an excellent opportunity to reconnect and interact—and people prefer to do business with people they know, like, and trust.

Prepared to do business as well as to have a wonderful experience—I got both! Old friendships were renewed by talking about "the good old days," and enhanced by the added dimension of talking about business.

If you are interested in business as well as pleasure at your reunion:

• Plan ways to initiate contact and follow through.

- Contact people before the reunion to show your interest in them.
- Practice an upbeat, interesting, concise introduction that includes something about your business.
- Ask for leads, and *offer* leads.

I'm not suggesting that you set up a card table just inside the door with your name flashing in neon above it. Don't overwhelm people with your information; just let them know what you do—when it is appropriate. Reunions can be a business gold mine, but there is no point in offending people with an inappropriate "hard sell." Besides, the first reason to attend any reunion is to "reunite" and have fun.

PREPARING FOR THE REUNION— A WEEK TO LOSE TWENTY POUNDS

Start preparing for your reunion *early*. You'll want more than a week to tackle those twenty pounds, and more than a few hours the morning your plane leaves to get yourself ready—physically, psychologically, and professionally. You'll work the room with ease and grace by preparing in advance:

- ATTITUDE. Go with the idea of having fun, and don't fret about what people will think of you. Remember, the best way to overcome self-consciousness is to concentrate on making others feel comfortable. No one attends a reunion without some second thoughts.

    "Being genuinely interested in people" should be no problem here. Who can resist wondering what has happened to the Prom Queen (now the mother of six), the class president (a jazz musician), the Serious

Student (a TV anchorwoman making six figures), or the Class Nerd (a software genius who could buy and sell everyone in the room six times over, and has also developed a charming personality)?

A friend recently attended her twenty-fifth *grammar* school reunion, and found herself talking with the Class Nerd. This guy used to stand 5'3" and weigh 100 pounds dripping wet, but a quarter of a century later was 6'2" and gorgeous. She remarked on how people had changed and he replied, rocking back and forth on his heels, "They sure have. Me? I discovered testosterone..."

Keep an open mind. A lot of nice things happen to people in twenty years, and it is a good idea give your old classmates a clean slate. Cliff probably doesn't throw spitballs in board meetings the way he did in history class. Mona may have sworn off hurtful gossip nineteen years ago.

And remember, you have nothing to prove. Be yourself and enjoy.

- FOCUS. Identify the people to whom you definitely want to talk about business, but be open to serendipity. Allow for the unplanned and the unexpected. That could mean a business referral or a romance. You never know what you'll find out about your old friends or their interests.

  During my visit to Chicago for the reunion, I went shopping at Marshall Fields—another reunion in itself! When the saleswoman heard why I was in town, she told me about her recent fortieth reunion. Two people, a widow and a widower, attended alone.

Within ten months they were married and had
moved to Miami!

One focus to avoid is proving to people how
much you've changed, or how successful you are.
These tactics usually backfire, and aren't much fun
anyway. The people who use them put themselves,
and other people, on trial.

Concentrate on the pleasure of connecting with
old friends in new ways...and don't worry if you've
put on .a few pounds in twenty years. Most of us
(certainly, those of us who have matured) know that
it isn't the cover that counts, it's the content.

• CARDS. I'll say it again. Don't leave home without
them. Not only do you avoid the wine-soaked napkin
routine, but exchanging cards leads to followup
correspondence and communication that renews
friendships.

Build your Millionaire's Rolodex, even if all your
contacts are purely social.

It's important to exercise good judgment and
good taste when handing out your cards. Shell
Norriss of Class Reunion, Inc. noticed one man at a
reunion who "arrived late and moved through the
banquet, dropping a handful of cards at each table."
I doubt that he received any business from such a
tacky tactic.

* * *

REUNION TIPS

A few miscellaneous tips about reunions:

1. *Spouses and Significant Others*: Leave home without him! Experts on reunions almost universally agree that husbands should be left at home. According to Judy Markey, "His presence will be classic third wheeldom."

You will notice the use of male pronouns. This is gender-biased and for good reason. The scientific studies aren't in yet, but empirical evidence suggests that while the "boys'" wives manage to fit in and even, in some cases, have a good time, the "girls'" husbands *suffer visibly*.

Perhaps this is because they aren't used to their wives being the center of attention, perhaps because they aren't accustomed to being schlepped to events as the "significant other," perhaps because the "boys" are fascinated to see the "girls" but could care less about their husbands. Who knows? What is increasingly evident, however, is that to bring your husband or male significant other to a reunion is to invite disaster. It will definitely put a damper on your good time.

There are exceptions, but they are rare. My restauranteur friend Rick Enos actually had fun at his wife's reunion because, "I never had to feel bad about forgetting a name or face."

David Peterson—then a significant other, now a spouse—had a terrific time at his wife's reunion. Peterson, legislative director of the Chicago Teachers' Union, offered, "I go out with the intention of having fun. I basically enjoy people and I felt the joy you all were having at your reunion."

Peterson could make a fortune giving seminars for other males on "how to be spouses." "Bride" training for men?

2. *Humor.* Bring a healthy sense of humor. If you can laugh at whatever gaffs or goofs you make, people will be more comfortable with you. No one liked being the butt of jokes or sarcastic remarks back in high school, and they are even less likely to enjoy it now. Perhaps Eddy didn't like being teased for "throwing like a girl" on the playground. Now that he owns a professional football team, he'll like it even less. And Debby got rid of her braces twenty years ago, so let's give her a break even though it was very funny when she kissed Arthur at the Junior Prom and they got stuck." She can bring it up, but be careful and ready to back off if *you* do.

3. *Talk to Everyone.* Our tastes and values have changed in twenty years, and so have *we*. Other people have changed, too. Move around the room and speak to everyone. You never know what treasure you'll find. The nerd of yesterday could be the nice guy of today...and tomorrow.

4. *Time Travel Tip.* If you travel "back home" for your family, high school or fraternity reunion, build in some time to reconnect with other old friends.

When I went back to Chicago, I planned separate get-togethers with my old college buddies. While there, I also took a deep breath, clenched my teeth and called my first college boyfriend, David Schultz, who is now an attorney in Chicago. I had not seen or spoken to him in eighteen years. Nothing ventured, nothing gained. What I gained was a dear friend and staunch supporter.

5. *Follow up.* Reunions are a wonderful networking opportunity both for friends and for business associations—but only if you follow up. It doesn't matter how significant

your connection over the punch bowl was. If you don't follow up, the opportunity is lost. That's just as true for social connections as it is for business contacts.

Take a few minutes to write notes to the people with whom you had particularly pleasant experiences. Let them know, at the very least, that you enjoyed seeing them again. If you want to go a step further and renew the relationship, suggest writing and/or getting together. And if you discussed business, by all means send them your brochure if you said you would...and any other information you think they might find interesting.

REMINDERS

Reunions are a chance to reunite with old friends and reestablish long-time connections...as well as to have a lot of fun and build your business network. Prepare ahead of time, do your homework, relax and enjoy while you are there, and follow up.

Connect with people as they are today. Some of the people from your past may be great prospects for your future—both personally and professionally.

Have a good time, and remember that anything can happen.

Chapter 12

WORKING THE
TRADE SHOW
OR CONVENTION:
THE TRADEOFFS

Chapter 12

Trade shows and conventions are the Olympics—the supreme test of your ability to work a room. As they say about New York, if you can make it there, you'll make it anywhere.

Not only do trade shows and conventions feature almost *all* the types of events we've discussed—business meetings, "social" gatherings, cocktail parties, dinners, lunches, individual encounters, and sometimes even reunions—but there are usually *hundreds* of these events, all crammed into the space of a few days to a week.

Some of the events on the schedule will be called "social," but make no mistake—this is business and requires the ability to work a room.

And it is work! Just ask anyone who has ever staffed a booth—standing! Or anyone who has walked through miles and miles of exhibits. Most women agree that the difficulty of these activities increases in direct proportion to the height of their heels.

But take heart. With a bit of planning and strategizing, trade shows and conventions can also be a tremendous amount of fun. After all, you are there to connect with people.

"Meeting your colleagues and friends is the most important aspect of a convention," says Tom Peters of *In Search of Excellence* and *A Passion for Excellence*.

Whether you attend the trade show or convention as an exhibitor, a potential buyer, a representative of the facility where it is taking place, a member of the organization, or simply as an interested party or the spouse of one of these people, certain strategies will help you get the most out of the event.

PREPARING FOR THE ONSLAUGHT

Most of us want to use our trade show/convention time (and money) wisely. Getting what we came for is important not only to us, but to our employers. The folks who paid for us to be there expect success. And if we're self-employed and have shelled out the money for the conference, booth, materials, air fare and expenses ourselves, the event had *better* be profitable.

The time to start preparing is *not* when the plane touches down or when we get our first peek at the convention hall. First of all, it is easy to be overwhelmed by the sheer volume of things—the number of people to see, booths to visit, meetings to attend, parties to drop in on, and by the immense physical distances to be covered. It's not unusual to attend six to eight events in the course of a day—and that's before the evening cocktail parties, drop-ins, dinners, hospitality suites, and late night get-togethers.

As the saying goes, "If you don't know where you're going, you're likely to wind up somewhere else."

Regardless of your role at the event, preparation is crucial. It should start long before you get on the plane. Jerry Westenhaver, General Manager of the Hyatt Regency in Oakland, believes that spending the time and effort to prepare saves time and money in the long run. "When I attend the Food and Beverage Trade Show or National Restaurant Association, I have a plan that reflects my general purpose and specific ideas and needs. There is so much information and machinery that without a plan it is difficult to accomplish anything."

Chris Carr, Director of Conference Services for the American Automobile Association, corroborates the need for a plan. "The attendees who find a trade show, convention or conference to be of value follow true to form. They go with the intention of gathering needed information, exploring products and services, and they map out a schedule. The old adage that applies here is, 'You get out what you put in'!"

Conventions and trade shows require a three-pronged approach to planning:

1. Planning for the office to run smoothly while you are away
2. Planning for the time spent at the event
3. Planning for follow-up

DON'T LEAVE HOME WITHOUT...
1. TAKING CARE OF THE FOLKS BACK HOME.
With all you'll have to do at the trade show or convention, you don't need to be worried about what's

happening back home—whether your mail and phones are being answered, whether someone remembered to cancel your dentist appointment, whether your clients are getting everything they need, whether someone is feeding your cat (and children!).

Make a list of the things for which you are responsible at the office and at home. You may have to delegate some projects or trade off some tasks, reschedule appointments, and train someone to handle your mail and phones the way you want them handled.

At home, your preparation may include lining up baby-sitters or housesitters, finding someone to care for your plants or pets, alerting your neighbors that you'll be gone, determining which bills need to be paid, cancelling the paper, getting someone to take in your mail, and the R.S.V.P. for a party that takes place just after you return.

Making these preparations not only lets you leave with comfort and enjoy the convention, but ensures that you won't come back to an overwhelming mess.

2. THINKING AHEAD TO THE EVENT.

You can eliminate a million distractions by anticipating your own needs at the convention—and the needs of others.

FIRST, get the facts straight—the dates, place, times, locations, and accommodations. Most groups send an advance schedule of events, and some include a map of the exhibits. If you can, plan your route through the convention hall in advance so that you can see the people you want to see without walking extra miles.

Be sure you understand the financial arrangements. Does your company pre-pay the costs? Is there an expense account for entertainment? Do you cover costs and present receipts for reimbursement? If you are self-employed, financial arrangements and allocations must be built into your business's budget.

SECOND, you need to understand exactly why you are attending this convention. Are you there to investigate the latest trends, developments or products? Are you being sent to gather data or information from the seminars, or to land new accounts? Will you be expected to report back? How detailed will your reports need to be? Is this a crash course for *you* to increase your skill, knowledge, and effectiveness? It is important that you make these determinations before you go.

If you are self-employed, you will have to make them for yourself. Before a recent convention of the National Speakers Association, I was telling a colleague, humorist Larry Wilde, that I was going through the membership list and writing notes to people with whom I wanted to meet, reconnect, or spend some extra time.

Larry suggested that I also write down all the questions I had about the speaking business at that point in my career, target the people I thought could answer those questions, and go prepared so that I would come away with exactly the information I needed. That was some of the best advice I've ever received. I did what Larry suggested, and it played an enormous part in making the convention a success for me.

Perhaps you are attending this conference simply to increase your contact base. Much of what is learned and accomplished at a convention may be done informally. Sometimes I've learned more chatting with a colleague or mentor over coffee than I would have by attending six seminars.

THIRD, plan your clothing. What you take will be determined by the location of the convention and the time of year. Find out what the weather is likely to be. Check the schedule to see if you'll need clothing for a meeting, an afternoon barbecue, a pool party, two cocktail hours, and a formal dinner on the same day.

Take clothes that are appropriate and comfortable. Shoes should be *especially* comfortable. You won't be able to work the show as effectively if you are hobbled by blisters or if your feet are screaming for a rest. You won't have as much fun, either.

And remember, this is business. See-through, backless, and frontless dresses are not acceptable. Nor are jeans for an awards banquet, in most cases.

FOURTH, be aware of the culture, norms and expected behaviors of the industry, profession or company. A convention of the National Rifle Association will have a different character than a trade show for pre-school educational toys. Different types of people will be present, and different behaviors will be expected. Know the world you're about to "work."

FIFTH, schedule your travel arrangements so that you have some time to relax and recover from jet lag before you "hit the floor." Don't plan to land at 2:00 and attend a 2:30 meeting. Why arrive harried and out of breath at the airport, the registration desk or the meeting when you could have a better time being gracious and serene?

Patricia Fripp, an international speaker who travels hundreds of thousands of miles a year, believes in Thorndike's Law: Performance that is rewarded, tends to be repeated. "This works for management and self-management," she says. Fripp rewards herself for arriving early at the airport by calling her friends and chatting. That way, the extra time isn't wasted; it's enjoyed. "The one time I cut it too tightly, naturally, was the time I locked my keys in the car! Now I build in 'catastrophe time' for freeway accidents and long lines at airport security."

And while we're on the subject of travel, remember that unforeseen circumstances always occur. Suitcases, boxes of materials, and airplanes often travel to different destinations. Henny Youngman tells this story: Checking in for a flight to Des Moines, the seasoned traveler told the airline employee, "Please send this red suitcase to Omaha, the blue one to Newark, and the box to Miami."

"Sir," the surprised employee replied, "we can't do that."

"Why not? That's what you did last week!"

Funny. . . sort of. Unless you are the traveler in question. Take your luggage. . . Please! At least take a carry-on with one change of clothing and underwear, plus toiletries and important papers.

SIXTH, remember the basics. Prepare a positive attitude. Know your focus—your purpose and goals for attending the convention or show. It helps to make a written plan. Work on your self-introduction and develop conversation starters appropriate to the event.

3. PLANNING TO FOLLOW-UP. Bring everything you will need to record expenses, take notes or tape seminars, collect and organize business cards, and gather follow-up information.

And of course, you will bring your own business cards and company brochures. Ruthe Hirsch of Ruth Hirsch Enterprises found the industry trade shows a superb forum for booking business. "I was always prepared to work all day at our booth and to follow up at the hospitality suites later that day. It was exhausting, but it was worthwhile," claims Hirsch.

"Follow-up is critical," according to Chris Carr of AAA, who plans thirty to thirty-five meetings per year. "I just attended a trade show and spoke to fifteen different companies about booking my conventions. Only *three* sent the follow-up material promised!"

Include yourself in your follow-up plans. Most people forget to plan for "Regroup and Recoup" time when they get home, but I have found this to be invaluable. Build in time to unpack, sort mail, do laundry, and just spend some "down" time before launching back into the routine. You've been in a completely different world, operating at a high pitch, and both need and deserve a mini-vacation—even if it's only a morning or an afternoon.

THERE'S GOLD IN THEM THAR BOOTHS

The booths at conventions and trade shows are golden opportunities, whether you are a buyer or seller. The whole point of booths is to bring large numbers of buyers and sellers together for their mutual benefit.

Whether you are behind the booth or in front of it, the *real* work occurs before you leave your office. Again, planning is the key. "Organization, attention to details and the ability to see the overall picture are essential to the planning and preparation," claims Debra Vogensen-Lentz, President of Eventions, a meeting and event planning company.

Jerry Westenhaver of the Hyatt Regency also says that pre-planning is essential. He works with his sales managers to establish both primary and secondary targets. "We take the time to learn about the association so that conversation flows more readily. It's too easy to talk to other purveyors or long-term clients. Our goal is to establish new relationships. Also, I reinforce for my staff that we cannot prejudge other attendees and must exhibit manners and extend our social graces to everyone."

Walking around the convention requires concentration and persistence. Faced with so many choices and so many people to see, it's easy to tune out, talk to whomever is around, and turn the show or convention into a continuous party rather than staying focused on the goals. Stay focused, and take short breaks if you need them.

According to a Tradeshow Bureau study reported in American Society of Association Executives' *Marketing Newsletter* (November 1985), 57% of all trade show attendees plan to buy one or more of the exhibited products or services within the year. The Newsletter also reports that it takes only one follow-up call to close a sale to a prospect met at a trade show, as opposed to five calls needed to close the average industrial sale. Why? "Because about 80% of the attendees typically are managers who influence purchase decisions."

But there is a catch. A marketing strategy must be planned before you attend. According to Howard Feiertag, Senior Vice President of Royce Resorts, a completed marketing plan will help target the appropriate trade show markets. That plan must also include the tactics which will be used and the goals established in terms of numbers of prospects and qualified leads.

For attendees, the trade show is a chance to research, assess and qualify products and services. It is also an educational experience, an opportunity to learn the state of the art, and a way to eliminate telephone tag because the exchange of information is instantaneous.

Being aware of the benefits helps us to work trade shows and conventions more effectively and expedite business from both sides of the booth.

WORKING THE BOOTH

Staff training is *paramount*. Your staff need to be well informed about the product or service they are selling, about the competition, and about how to draw business to the booth.

When they only know about their product, and haven't bothered to research the attendees who are potential buyers, they lose sales. Chris Carr of AAA says, "It is disconcerting as an association executive, when you have a budget to spend on a product or service, or need a site for a convention and the booth personnel can only speak of 'corporate' needs."

Homework works. It produces good connections, satisfaction, sales, and good feelings for everyone involved.

THE THREE E'S

The people behind the booths should also exhibit The Three E's—Effort, Energy and Enthusiasm—according to Pam Massarsky, Secretary of the Illinois Teachers Union, who has worked both sides of the booth.

Your staff should prepare interesting tidbits as conversation starters. Since everyone at the show or convention will have a nametag, your people might open with a question or comment about the company and/or its location. They should also prepare questions about the attendees' needs or the suppliers' products and services. And they should listen to the answers.

"May I help you?" is *not* a good opener for the exhibitor. It gives the attendee a perfect chance to say, "No thanks, I'm just looking." That closes the discussion; anything the exhibitor says after that might be construed as a "hard sell." They might as well be discussing shirts in Macy's.

"May I help you?" should be asked only at candy stores—where the customers are pre-sold. If you walk into Fanny Mae's or See's, you're not looking for Whitman's Sampler. You're there to buy Fanny Mae's or See's, and the only choice is between Tipperary Bon Bons or Walnut Squares!

A firm handshake, a smile, warmth, and a (practiced) upbeat self-introduction will make the initial contact easier and more effective.

BOOTH DESIGN

Booth design is also important. Your booth should be attractive and capture interest. Westenhaver says that a gimmick can be useful if it has mass appeal. "At the last trade show, we had a shoe shine booth. As our sales managers shined shoes, they had two or three minutes to speak with potential clients. We *really* worked our booth...and we had fun!"

Nancy Shina, Corporate Director of Sales for Quality Inns International, uses an interesting tactic. She believes that many booths are designed to create barriers. "Because the table can make the solicitation process intimidating for the buyer, we moved the six-foot table to the side, removing the barrier. The result was that the flow into the booth increased."

The unusual and original always make a booth more interesting. Dick Shaff, General Manager at San Francisco's Moscone Convention Center, says, "Because we want to convey the hospitality of San Francisco as EVERYONE'S FAVORITE CITY, our exhibit is a 40' x 40' living room with a pianist. The people who staff our booth are good communicators who are well-versed in a segment of our convention or trade show services."

THE THREE S'S

Joe Jeff Goldblatt owns the Wonder Company, which produces special events, conventions and corporate meetings. He says, "trade shows and meetings are THEATER for which you must know the SCRIPT, SCHEDULE and STAGING. The script is that body of information you must give and receive. The schedule refers to the timetable as well as the appointments set *prior* to the event. Staging is equally important; you must know when and where to move. An off-peak-hours visit to exhibits or an early arrival at a general session provide excellent opportunities to meet colleagues. People prefer to do business with reputable, qualified friends."

* * *

WALKING THE FLOOR

When you go around to see other people's exhibits, you'll want to be at your best. Here are some tips for conserving energy so that you can sparkle while you mingle and converse:

- Map out your route before you begin so that you are sure to see the people you must see.
- Don't try to do too much in one day, and arrive at the last booth looking (and feeling) as if you've just run the marathon.
- Make a list of people you want to see, and things you want to do, and carry it with you.
- Carry a small notebook with you to jot down information and ideas.
- Resist the temptation to take everyone's brochure, gift, and hand-out. You could be carrying an extra fifty pounds by the time you work your way around the room.
- Stick as closely as you can to your normal regimens for food and exercise. If you are used to working out each day, you may begin to wilt if you don't incorporate this into your routine. Some conferences schedule early morning runs to accommodate joggers —and they are also a good place to meet people. Many conference facilities have tennis courts, weight rooms, and saunas on the premises. Be aware of what kinds of foods and eating schedules allow you to function best. If you need a big breakfast, have one. But if you are grumpy in the morning, it might be a

good idea to order from room service. Take care of yourself. Honoring your own routine is very important.

CONVENTIONAL CHARM

At trade shows and conventions, business isn't always conducted around the booth. The "social" aspects of these events are just as important. I put "social" in quotation marks because if you are at a trade show or convention, *you are working.* But that doesn't mean you can't enjoy yourself, meet new people, reconnect with those you know, and extend yourself to everyone around you.

"I believe in being social," says Kris Harp, Sales Manager for the Oakland Convention & Visitors Bureau. I see trade shows as an opportunity to meet people, determine needs and most of all, establish rapport...the foundation for ongoing working relationships."

These events are made to order for increasing your base of contacts. Make an effort to sit with people you don't know at dinners and luncheons. Take the initiative and introduce yourself to the people at your table. Ask them to do the same, just as you might at your local professional association dinner meeting. Carl La Mell of the Victor Neumann Association did this and met a man across the table who presented his card and told La Mell to call if he ever needed his service. Eight months later, that man arranged a $450,000 loan so that La Mell's association could purchase its building.

The "social" parts of the trade show or convention can be just as fun, and just as profitable, as working the convention floor.

* * *

TRADE SHOW TEMPTATIONS— TRYSTING AND TIPPLING

There are a few social aspects of the trade show or convention that bear some warning.

The trade show tryst is a touchy issue. Miscommunication can make for uncomfortable situations. Be conscious of the verbal and nonverbal messages you send. Be clear what you want, and what you don't. Your boss sent you in good faith to represent the organization. Will an "indiscretion" get back to him or her—or to the other people in the office? How would this be received? How would *you* be perceived? Yes, you have a personal life and are entitled to privacy. But at a conference, you are still on company time. Maybe mother's "conventional" wisdom has a place here: "May all your 'affairs' be catered."

Drinking is another delicate subject. Sloppy behavior is usually offensive, and can mean losing a client, or even a job. Know your limits. Women are not expected to "keep up with the guys" around cocktail hour. So don't. Looking like you're ravaged by a hangover the next morning won't impress anyone.

Convention behavior requires alertness, an ability to listen and comprehend, and the capacity to give out information selectively. If liquor impairs any of these three areas, you will be less effective.

One man I know has a rule: None of his salespeople can drink before 6:00 p.m., and they have a two-drink limit. He, on the other hand, positions himself at the bar by 10:00 a.m. with orange juice on the rocks. He buys screwdrivers for everyone, acting as the congenial host and listening carefully to what everyone says. By the end of the day, he has learned many secrets—about the industry and about his competitors. By sticking to straight OJ, he controls the information he gives out—and never catches a cold at a conference!

Let common sense be the rule of thumb. Attend the sessions, learn, make personal and professional contacts, and secure clients. Take notes, buy tapes, visit the exhibit hall and analyze the products for your boss. *Then* decide what you want to do for relaxation.

That doesn't mean you can't have fun. You can. A convention is a *balance* of work and play. Don't be a stick in the mud, but remember that conventions can easily turn into three-day office parties—and some office parties can come back to haunt you.

The balancing act here is to keep your sense of humor without losing your perspective.

SPOUSES— TIRED OF GETTING SCHLEPPED ALONG?

It's not easy to go to an event where you are identified only as someone's spouse. Unless you are blessed with an abundance of the Dynamic Duo—chutzpah and charm— and make it your business to *start* fascinating conversations that are of interest to you, they always don't happen.

At one time, most of the spouses at conventions were wives who did not work outside the home. All that has changed. Now about 45% of the spouses who attend conventions work outside the home. At a recent American College of Surgeons Convention in San Francisco, 10% of the attendees at programs for spouses were male.

Joyce Siegel, who has attended medical conventions and meetings for more than forty years, has observed this shift. "More and more, we see on the name badges that the doctor is female and the spouse is male. And the programs offered to us have changed. Flower-arranging programs have been replaced by estate and tax planning and time management."

Spouses must know how to work a room, too, so that they feel their time has been invested wisely. Gary McBee, Executive Vice President of Pacific Bell, believes that his wife Chris' friendliness has helped him to overcome his reserve. "She enjoys people and they enjoy her. It's a very special quality to have."

But some spouses enjoy socializing more than others. What does *not* work is to bring (or be) a Sullen Spouse, one who doesn't really enjoy either mingling or the convention itself. These spouses can often support their husband or wife best by staying home and doing the things they do enjoy.

A TRADE SHOW TRIUMPH

I know from experience that unless you're famous, or infamous, getting a book published can be a challenge.

My friend Jean Miller, a former librarian, knew I was writing a book. When the American Library Association Convention came to San Francisco, she suggested I attend because every publisher in the country, large or small, would be there. Although Jean had already visited the convention, she consented to go again with me.

When the day came, I had a virus. I felt awful and didn't want to go. The thought of getting dressed up, organizing my materials, driving to Moscone Center, and walking through miles of exhibits seemed like torture. I couldn't imagine working up the energy to approach people, converse, establish rapport, and maybe spark their interest in my book.

I told Jean I just couldn't do it. She was sympathetic, but reminded me that it was "quite an opportunity." MY OWN WORDS, come back to haunt me. I went.

As we walked through the exhibit area, the Shapolsky Publishers booth caught Jean's eye and she insisted that I speak to him. Ian Shapolsky and I chatted and made a connection. I sent him a proposal, and he talked to my agent.

You are holding the result in your hands.

This story is about a trade show triumph, but it's also about the value of spending time with people who support you and your goals. Jean not only pointed me in the right direction, quite literally; she coaxed me toward my goals even when I was not feeling well.

REMINDERS

The trade show or convention is a unique opportunity to increase your base of contacts, to buy and sell products and services, and to have fun. Where else could you find so many rooms to work in one place at one time? This is the big time, the marathon, the ultimate challenge to those of us who value the ability to work a room.

To get the most out of it and keep from being overwhelmed, plan in advance:

1. The smooth running of the office while you are away
2. Your work at the convention itself
3. Your follow-up

Working a booth or an entire trade show is just like working a room—only more so! Rise to the challenge, seize the golden opportunity, and have fun!

Chapter 13

WORKING THE WORLD: TRAINS & BOATS & PLANES, ETC.

Chapter 13

It's a fact of life: People who know how to work a room produce more results and have more fun. You have the skills now, and may have started enjoying the benefits already. Why limit your ability to work a room to meetings, dinners, cocktail parties, business lunches and formal social engagements?

Why not make every situation you encounter a "room" and WORK THE WORLD? The worst that can happen is that you enjoy life more, and the chances are good that you'll also make new friends and improve your business.

THE CORNUCOPIA OF CONTACTS

What is a room? Whatever you *make* it! It can be:
• The Airplane
• The Golf Course
• The Pool
• The Bowling Alley
• The Bleachers at the Ballpark
• The Nightclub or Theater
• The Jogging Track

- The Supermarket
- The Department Store
- The Bike Shop
- The Sushi Bar
- The Hardware Store
- The Bank
- Anywhere You Go

You don't go to these places in order to 'work' them, but as long as you have to stand in line at the supermarket, why not have a pleasant conversation? Will it bring you a business deal? Who knows? That's not the point. The point is to extend yourself to people, be open to whatever comes your way, and have a good time in the process. One never knows.

Obviously, you have to exercise some caution. There are certain parts of town you probably don't want to work—especially at night. But what could it hurt to strike up a conversation with the man who works in the hardware store? You might just learn how to use that complicated VCR function that's been baffling you for two years!

CHANCE ENCOUNTERS

Planes are great places to meet people. You have a captive audience. I met one of the most significant people in my life on a plane from San Francisco to Los Angeles. Fr. Larry Lorenzoni, now at the Vatican, and I spent an hour chatting, laughing, comparing publications, and enjoying a meeting of the minds and spirits...on a higher plane, of course. What if I hadn't taken the risk and spoken to him?

* * *

A MARRIAGE MADE IN HEAVEN

Clare Revelli, designer and author of the bestselling book and video *Color and You*, was flying home to San Francisco after a grueling business trip to New York. Airports all over the East were closed down, and 40,000 Christmas travelers were stranded at O'Hare. As she changed planes and took her seat in First Class, Clare observed chaos and hysteria. Grown men were hiding in the lavatories to 'catch' a ride home. People were pushing and yelling as they boarded the plane." Just as the jetway was closing, a man boarded and was told to sit anywhere. He walked down the aisle toward the vacant seat next to Clare.

"His warm and happy smile greeted me, eliciting a kind of spiritual, yet romantic reaction. He was almost magical, reflecting such peacefulness in the midst of pandemonium; such ease in the crush of chaos. The next four and a half hours were heavenly and we knew then we would spend our lives together. About a year later I became Mrs. Grant August Schieldt and believe ours was a marriage made in heaven (or 37,000 feet)."

Not everyone is as lucky as Clare. Sometimes a seatmate would rather spend the time with his or her own thoughts or a good book. Allow for the busy or preoccupied person and respect his wishes.

There is no room for Mr. or Ms. Sleaze in working the world. A phony friendliness or the appearance that someone is trying to make their Contact Quota is all the more obvious when that person is trying to work the world.

* * *

COMMON GROUND

What is unique about working the world is that there is always a clear common ground. Wherever you are, the people there with you are in the same situation.

If you are on the golf course, the common interest is golf. Keith Goto is an avid golfer from Honolulu, and most of the conversations he has with people he meets on courses across the United States center around golf. He rarely mentions his position as Vice-President of a Fortune 500 company. He lets his golf game speak for him. And since he usually shoots in the 70's, his score says a lot. "I have met people on the course who have become golfing buddies and friends," Goto says. "Because of golf, I have been the Chairperson of the Multiple Sclerosis Tournament for three years. Although I was so busy I played a little less golf, it felt good to contribute to a worthy cause while organizing a tournament for my fellow golfers."

If you are at the jogging track, the other people will probably be joggers as well—or thinking about becoming joggers. If you are at the ice cream store, everyone else will be just as interested in a cone, a scoop, or a sundae as you are. You might even compare notes on flavors.

Once after a convention, I went down to the hotel pool and was practicing my "swimming," which is what I call my novice attempts to move forward in water without my feet touching bottom. The only other person in the pool was a man who was swimming laps, breathing underwater, and doing all sorts of impressive things. I happened to mention to him that I didn't swim. The result: he worked with me for an hour and a half and taught me how to swim. Wonderful things come to you when you work the world!

The contacts you make while working the world may or may not evolve into friendships or business associates. You may never see these people again. Even if you don't, you've brightened your own day and someone else's with the encounter.

But sometimes these connections resurface when we least expect it. Three years ago, I met John Sneed on an airplane from San Francisco to New Orleans. We chatted and laughed for four hours—and stayed in touch.

He wanted me to contact his sister, a marketing director for a public accounting firm and a fellow ex-teacher, but for one reason or another it never happened. Two years later I was giving a seminar in her city and John suggested again that I contact her. I did, and she hired me to do a seminar for her firm.

Sometimes these connections are profound, and sometimes they are fleeting but pleasant. When my friend Lisa Miller was doing research on the best bike to buy, the manager of a local bike shop introduced her to another biker who also happened to operate a bakery. A few weeks later, she needed a birthday cake for a friend. She decided to visit his shop, and he was behind the counter. "Ordinarily, I would have smiled, placed my order and left. . .*wishing* I had said something to him. But this time, I took a deep breath and reintroduced myself. He did remember meeting me in the bike shop. The reward for taking a risk: great service and a delicious, free cookie!"

* * *

THIS IS YOUR LIFE

Each of us has a similar story, an example of how circumstances and connections evolved into something wonderful. It doesn't happen by accident; it happens because we exert energy.

They say "You can't give a smile away; it always comes back." The same is true of a kind word or a conversation starter. What goes around, comes around.

Seize the moment, wherever you are. Smile and say something. . .anything! Practice striking up conversations. As with everything else you practice, it will get easier and you'll get better at it.

The benefits are the best life has to offer—connections with other people. In a sense, "working the world" is just another way of saying "living life to the fullest."

The rewards go to the risk-takers, those who are willing to put their egos on the line and reach out—to other people and to a richer, fuller life for themselves.

That is what this book has been about—reaching out. Success in business is nice, but connecting with people is nicer. Working the world, and your life, should bring you both.

Chapter 14

THE GOSPEL ACCORDING TO ROANE: THE TEN COMMANDMENTS OF CONNECTING

Chapter 14

1. THOU SHALT PREPARE:
   Attitude, focus, self-introduction, conversation, business cards, smile and handshake

2. THOU SHALT ATTEND:
   R.S.V.P. and Go! Act like a gracious host.

3. THOU SHALT TRY STRATEGIES THAT FEEL COMFORTABLE:
   Read nametags, Go with a buddy. Talk to white-knuckled drinkers. Approach and be approachable. Smile. Allow for serendipity. Listen. Care. Extricate courteously and circulate gracefully. Follow up. Call or send "thank you's."

4. THOU SHALT SAY SOMETHING...ANYTHING:
   Don't wait; initiate. Take the risk; the rewards are yours. Listen with interest to the response. Smile and make eye contact.

5. THOU SHALT MIND THY MANNERS:
   Learn old and new etiquette and brush up on your manners. Acknowledge others. Treat *everyone* nicely.

6. THOU SHALT AVOID THE COMMON
   CRUTCHES:
   Do not arrive too late. Don't leave too early. Don't drink
   too much. Don't gorge at the buffet table. Don't misuse
   the buddy system by joining yourselves at the hip.

7. THOU SHALT REMEMBER THE THREE E'S:
   Make an EFFORT.
   Bring your ENERGY.
   Exude ENTHUSIASM.

8. THOU SHALT DRESS APPROPRIATELY:
   Unsure? Ask!

9. THOU SHALT REMEMBER THE FOUR C'S:
   COURTESY
   CARING
   CHARM
   CHUTZPAH

10. THOU SHALT BRING THY SENSE OF HUMOR:
    Use the A.T.& T. Test (Appropriate, Tasteful, & Timely)

GLOSSARY
AND
REFERENCES

Glossary

The following are some of the terms I've used in the book plus a couple of others that you may find useful and/or amusing. I acknowledge Leo Rosten's *The Joys of Yiddish*.

CHUTZPAH -   Classic usages: Gall, brazen, nerve
              RoAne's usage: Gutsiness, courage
              (It takes a dose of chutzpah to
              initiate conversations.)

KIBBITZ -   To joke, fool around; to socialize
              aimlessly. (The group in the corner
              of the room were kibbitzing over
              coffee.)

KVETCH -   To fuss, gripe, complain. (I can't
              stand going out with Mary; she's
              constantly kvetching about one
              thing or another.)

KLUTZ -   A clod; a graceless person. (Run a
              marathon? I am such a klutz I'm

lucky if I can walk off a curb without spraining my ankle.)

MAVEN   An expert; knowledgeable person. (The "manners mavens" are every-increasing.)

NOSH   A snack; a-small portion; anything eaten between meals or "grazed." (I get so hungry by 4:00 p.m., I have to have a nosh to tide me over till dinner.)

NUDZH   Nudge; pester; nag; a surreptitious reminder of a job to be done. (Sara keeps nudzhing me to leave the party.)

SCHLEPP   To drag, pull, or lag behind. (They schlepped me all over town.)

SCHMOOZE   Friendly, gossipy, prolonged heart-to-heart talk or chit-chat. (John is glib. You always see him schmoozing with the guests at ever party.)

TUMULT   Noise, commotion. (The noise level was so high that the tumult interfered with conversation.)

References

Alihan, Milla, *Corporate Etiquette* (New York: Mentor, 1970).

Babcock, Judy, "Etiquette, Manners; Boor No More," *Success* (June, 1984) pp. 42-43.

Baldrige, Letitia, *Amy Vanderbilt's Everyday Etiquette*, (New York: Bantam, 1981).

Baldrige, Letitia, *Letitia Baldrige's Complete Guide to Executive Manners*. (Rawson Associates, 1985).

Butler, Pamela E., *Talking To Yourself*, (San Francisco: Harper & Row, 1981).

Feiertag, Howard, "Sales Clinic," *Hotel & Motel Management* (March, 1985) p. 44.

Givens, David, "The Animal Art of Getting Along," *Success* (April, 1985).

Goleman, Daniel, "People Can Often Judge How They Impress Others," *New York Times*, June 30, 1987, p. 14.

Goleman, Daniel, "Social Anxiety: New Focus Leads to Insight and Therapy," *New York Times*, December 18, 1984, p. C-1.

Hobhouse, Janet, "Blah, Blah, Blah," *Vogue* (April, 1986) p. 32.

Jaffe, Elliot, "Getting Chutzpah," *Savvy* (November, 1982) pp. 34-38.

Kennedy, Marilyn Moats, *Kennedy's Career Strategist* (February, 1986).

Keyfitz, Nathan, "The Baby Boom Meets the Computer Revolution," *American Demographics* (May, 1984), pp. 23-25, 45-46.

Korda, Michael, "Small Talk," *Signature*, September, 1986, p. 78.

Markey, Judy, *How to Survive Your High School Reunion and Other Mid-Life Crises* (Contemporary Books, 1985).

Martin, Judith, Numerous syndicated "Miss Manners" articles.

Minninger, Joan, *Total Recall: How to Boost Your Memory Power*, (New York: Pocket Books, 1984).

Morris, James, *The Art of Conversation* (New York: Cornerstone Library, 1976).

RoAne, Susan, "Career Series: Paying Up Pays Off," *San Francisco Examiner*, August 30, 1982.

RoAne, Susan, "Conventional Wisdom," *Executive Female* (September/October, 1982).

RoAne, Susan, "The RSVP Problem," *Meeting Manager (September,1985)*.

RoAne, Susan, *"How to Turn a Reunion into Business Breakthrough,"* San Jose Mercury News*, September 7, 1986.

RoAne, Susan, "How to Work a Trade Show," *Meeting Manager* (March, 1986).

Rosten, Leo, *The Joys of Yiddish* (New York: Washington Square Press, 1968).

Marcia Saft, "Professor Treats Problem of Shyness," *New York Times*, February 3, 1985, p. 4.

Schwartz, David J., *Magic of Thinking Big* (New York: Cornerstone Library, 1986).

637 of the Best Things Anybody Ever Said, collected and

arranged by Robert Byrne (New York: Fawcett Crest, 1981).

Walters, Barbara, *How to Talk with Practically Anybody About Practically Anything* (New York: Dolphin Books, 1983).

Susan RoAne,
keynote speaker and seminar leader, is founder of The RoAne
Group. Susan's presentations, which she has given for
associations, Fortune 500 companies, and universities, are
known for their practical information, results and humor.

For further information about Susan RoAne's programs,
contact:

Susan RoAne
The RoAne Group
14 Wilder St. #100
San Francisco, CA 94131
(415) 239-2224

Notes

Notes

Notes

Notes